Cryptocur

*A Simple Guide to Lear
Investing in Bitcoin Cash, _. ,,
Blockchains*

Mark Archer

© **Copyright 2020 by (Mark Archer) - All rights reserved.**

This document is geared towards providing exact and reliable information in regards to the topic and issue covered. The publication is sold with the idea that the publisher is not required to render accounting, officially permitted, or otherwise, qualified services. If advice is necessary, legal or professional, a practiced individual in the profession should be ordered.

- From a Declaration of Principles which was accepted and approved equally by a Committee of the American Bar Association and a Committee of Publishers and Associations.

In no way is it legal to reproduce, duplicate, or transmit any part of this document in either electronic means or in printed format. Recording of this publication is strictly prohibited and any storage of this document is not allowed unless with written permission from the publisher. All rights reserved.

The information provided herein is stated to be truthful and consistent, in that any liability, in terms of inattention or otherwise, by any usage or abuse of any policies, processes, or directions contained within is the solitary and utter responsibility of the recipient reader. Under no circumstances will any legal responsibility or blame be held against the publisher for any reparation, damages, or monetary loss due to the information herein, either directly or indirectly.

Respective authors own all copyrights not held by the publisher.

The information herein is offered for informational purposes solely, and is universal as so. The presentation of the information is without contract or any type of guarantee assurance.

The trademarks that are used are without any consent, and the publication of the trademark is without permission or backing by the trademark owner. All trademarks and brands within this book are for clarifying purposes only and are the owned by the owners themselves, not affiliated with this document.

Disclaimer:

This book contains neither recommendations nor solicitations to buy or sell securities and it is published solely for information and education purposes and does not form the basis of any contract or commitment whatsoever.

The author and the publisher assume no responsibilities for actions taken by readers, they do not provide investment advice and they do not make any claims, promises, or guarantees that any suggestions, system, information, trading strategies and/or etc. will result in a profit, or any other desired result.

All readers assume all risks, including but not limited to the risk of losses.

Cryptocurrency investments are risky. They do not provide fixed returns and past performances do not guarantee any future results.

All securities investments entail the risk of great and sudden financial losses. Returns may vary and you may have a loss when you decide to sell your securities. The expressed analysis and projections are subject to change without notice.

Table of content

INTRODUCTION: 7

CHAPTER 1: UNDERSTANDING CRYPTOCURRENCY: DAWN OF A NEW ECONOMY 11

1.1 What does cryptocurrency, Blockchain, and crypto trading mean? The basics 14

1.2 How a Blockchain works? 21

1.3 Exploring the Market of cryptocurrency 25

1.4 What do you need to know about cryptocurrency 28

CHAPTER 2: CLASSIFICATION OF CRYPTOCURRENCIES 34

2.1 What is a Bitcoin? 35

2.2 What are ALT coins and Tokens? 38

2.3 Bitcoin and beyond: the 10 cryptocurrencies with the highest market capitalization 43

CHAPTER 3: OPERATING CRYPTOCURRENCY 46

3.1 Role of Users, Miners, Exchanges, Trading Platforms, Wallet providers, Coin Inventors, and Coin offerors? 46

3.2 What is cryptocurrency mining? 50

3.3 Who are the key players? 52

CHAPTER 4: CRYPTOCURRENCY TRADING AND INVESTING 56

4.1 What is the value of cryptocurrencies, how are prices determined, and what could Bitcoin be worth in the future? 57

4.2 How to Invest in Cryptocurrency 67

4.3 How to start buying Bitcoins, Ethereum and other Altcoins 71

4.4 How to make money with cryptocurrencies? 76

4.5 How to store and track them once you have bought them 80

4.6 When to buy and sell? 86

4.7 Asset allocation and how much to invest in cryptocurrencies 93

4.8 What is ICO (Initial Coin offering)? 95

4.9 Is Cryptocurrency Taxable? 97

CHAPTER 5: STRATEGIES 100

5.1 What are the typical investment strategies? 100

5.2 Which investment strategy is right for me? 104

CHAPTER 6: OPINION ABOUT CRYPTOCURRENCY 106

6.1 What the Pros Think About Crypto 106

6.2 Are there any drawbacks to investing in cryptocurrencies? 109

6.3 The future of cryptocurrency and SEED VENTURE case study 112

6.4 Is it too late to get into cryptocurrencies – have you missed the boat? 117

6.5 Can crypto save the world? 118

7: CONCLUSION 120

8: REFERENCES 123

Introduction:

There's enormous interest in cryptocurrency space right now and ambiguity, uncertainty, and doubt on equal parts. Bitcoin, Cryptocurrencies, ICOs, blockchain. What does it even mean? The natural response to these general ideas is generally cynicism and dismissal, but there is a powerful new technology underneath the jargon that is revamping our financial system.

Cryptocurrencies are digital cash designed to be quicker, cheaper, and more reliable than money issued by our regular government. Instead of trusting a government to create the funds and banks to store, send, and receive it, users directly transact to each other and save their own money. Without an intermediary, people can send money instantly; transactions are typically very cheap and fast.

Cryptocurrencies with public records don't allow you to trust a bank to hold your money. We don't demand that you believe the person with whom you are doing business to pay you. Alternatively, you can see the money that thousands of people send, receive, check, and register. This system does not require trust. This unique positive quality is called trust lessness.

Bitcoin emerged as an innovation within the depths of the 2008 global financial crisis aimed at building a better financial system. Early on, cryptocurrencies formed a seedy undertone since they were primarily associated with black market trades: drug trafficking, ransomware transfers, money laundering, and tax evasion. Since the internet, cryptocurrency has been portrayed as the most disruptive technology, as well as a scam or substantial Ponzi scheme.

The critics say it's a speculative bubble, but for those who haven't found the right theories, that's just a simple out. We have the merits of asking the right questions but ultimately fail to identify the main reasons behind the fast-growing crypto-currency appetite. Bitcoin and other crypto-assets are an emerging new asset class witnessing rapid growth as a new technology that is fundamentally creative.

We are living in a digital world where the new generation enjoys trusting the "abstract," challenging traditional norms, and finding a stronger technical way forward. Bitcoin gives the world a multifunctional financial utility through the development of an open financial system, allowing us to store and exchange capital in ways we never before thought possible.

Bitcoin is digital money which nobody issues or regulates. It is used in anywhere in the world to store and move any amount of value securely. It is used for buying goods and services, holding resources, or giving money to anyone without a third party's permission. Sometimes called "Virtual Gold," an adequately stored bitcoin can't be hacked, stolen, or confiscated by a government. It is, therefore, giving full ownership to people, much like getting a Swiss bank account in their wallet. Like physical gold, Bitcoin can store or send anywhere in the world cheaper, quicker, and more secure. Bitcoin is divisible by the eighth decimal position, and is fully digital, allowing any monetary value to be transferred. Unlike the government's "fiat" currencies, which can be manipulated and devalued, a limited supply of 21 million bitcoins makes it a scarce and precious commodity. Bitcoin is money the internet and will do what the internet has done for communication to finance.

The Bitcoin network is a peer-to-peer network operating on a self-clearing distributed; decentralized ledger called the blockchain. Currency units operating on the Bitcoin network are called bitcoins, which are used to store and distribute value between participants in the system. Unlike most central bank-issued currencies that can be devalued and manipulated, bitcoins are distributed under a set of rules to produce sound money that can't be managed by a central authority or malicious actor. Users may purchase or sell goods and services, send money to people or organizations or even quickly, safely, and borderless extend credit. The only prerequisite for accessing these coins is an internet connection and a private key that provides access to the coins deposited on the Bitcoin network by forming a pair of public-facing keys. Unauthorized access to a private key for someone is equivalent to stealing gold from their safe.

Gold has long been considered the primary store of wealth. Today people turn to cryptocurrencies because they are safer, more comfortable to store and transport, more straightforward to use, and easier to subdivide than any established commodity today. It disrupts international payments and transfers business by cutting out banks/intermediaries' exorbitant fees, the global remittance industry (people working in one country and sending money back to their families), as well as becoming the internet currency and sparking a new wave of global e-commerce.

Why you should invest in anything for the same purposes, you should own some bitcoin: preserving or increasing your living standards over time. This is particularly important considering the inflationary pressures and the fact that fiat currencies are a lousy store of value. Everyone should create a diversified portfolio to protect their financial futures and help them to attain what they want most in life. Crypto-assets will play an essential role in that as experts think Bitcoin and blockchain-based assets are one of the most significant technological advances and will mark the most fabulous wealth generation event of our time.

Bitcoin and other crypto-assets valuations have gone up considerably, but we are still in long-term reasonably early stages. The best strategy is to use dollar-cost averaging to average the market, which minimizes the risk of market timing.

Cryptocurrency is explored and explained in a more comprehensive form in the upcoming parts of this book, including how it functions, and various investment strategies to optimize return on investment.

Chapter 1: Understanding cryptocurrency: Dawn of a new economy

Cryptocurrencies have drawn quite a lot of interest lately. You can find them mentioned regularly on the news, from a relative, or on Netflix.

Cryptocurrencies became the town's talk of late! A large number of people talk about cryptocurrencies, buy them, sell them-or invest.

There comes another word, Blockchain, which we often hear. Those new words have changed the whole situation in the investment world and have implemented several new ways of investing in new technologies.

Carrying out the proper research on cryptocurrencies may require that a prospective investor explore many areas. One area in particular which might prove helpful is merely learning the terminology of the primary industry. This dialect is particularly specific to the digital currency, making it unlikely to have been picked up by traders while researching certain asset classes such as stocks, shares, and commodities.

Once we start with the basic knowledge of these, let's get to know the primary language and words used in the cryptocurrency environment first.

Address: In digital currency, an address is simply a destination where a user sends digital currency and receives it. In a way, it's close to a bank account. Typically, such addresses contain a long series of letters and numbers.

Altcoin: An altcoin is an alternative digital currency to bitcoin.

Arbitrage: Throughout crypto, arbitrage refers to profiting from the price difference between two different exchanges.

ATH: "ATH" refers to the abbreviation "all-time high." To monitor digital currency markets, this word can be quite helpful.

Bear / Bearish: "Bears" believe the value of an asset, e.g., a digital currency, would decline. Another way to put that is that if an investor feels a cryptocurrency will depreciate, their feeling is "bearish" around the digital asset.

Blocks: Most digital currencies make use of blocks that contain transactions that have been verified and then combined.

Bull / Bullish: If an investor believes an asset will rise in value, he or she is a "bull."

Consensus: The network for a digital currency reaches agreement when the nodes of the system agree that a transaction has taken place.

Cryptocurrency: A cryptocurrency is merely a currency on which cryptography is based. For example, Bitcoin leverages cryptography for verification of transactions.

Cryptography: Cryptography is the process of encoding and decoding information to prevent would-be observers from understanding the data sent.

Exchanges: Exchanges are necessarily merely marketplaces where traders can exchange digital currency. If an individual wants to buy bitcoin, then heading to a transaction is the easiest way to achieve this target.

FOMO: The term ' FOMO' stands for the phrase ' fear of missing out.' This happens when investors start buying up a specific asset based on their expectations that it will increase in value.

Fork: A fork is a change in the rules or protocol regulating the digital currency.

FUD: Fear, uncertainty, and doubt can be summed up using the term "FUD." The idea behind this is that market participants may disseminate misleading or inaccurate information to cause the price of an asset to fall.

HODL: Cryptocurrency investors have developed the term 'HODL,' which stands for' hold on for dear life.' Digital currencies can become extremely volatile, so when they begin to experience significant price fluctuations, some market participants say they should simply' HODL.'

Initial Coin Offering (ICO): An initial coin offering (ICO) is the first time an organization offers digital tokens to the pub.

The market cap: The market cap for market capitalization, which is a word for total market value, is short. For example, the market cap of bitcoin is the amount of outstanding BTCs, multiplied by the price of the digital currency. The word may also be used to refer to a digital currency group.

Mining: Mining is the process of creating a digital currency with new units. For example, each time a block is mined, the bitcoin network releases new bitcoins.

Moon / Mooning: This means it increases dramatically in value when the digital currency sets. For example, a crypto-trader might speak about how an altcoin goes "to the moon!" industry insiders also characterize

Noob: Newcomers are described as "noobs" by the industry insiders

Satoshi Nakamoto: Satoshi Nakamoto is the alias for bitcoin's founder, and more than one person stated to be Nakamoto.

Token: A digital symbol is a digital currency device, like a bitcoin.

Whale: The term "whale" is used to describe a trader who makes sizable bets.

White Paper: Usually, developers who create digital currencies provide white papers for those innovative assets. Such documents typically offer comprehensive information on the related digital token and its underlying tech.

The cryptocurrency world is rushing, so there is no time to waste. Let's continue and discuss this new world of investment in the upcoming units in more detail.

1.1 What does cryptocurrency, Blockchain, and crypto trading mean? The basics

What is Cryptocurrency?

The short and easy answer to the question about the title is that cryptocurrency is digital money, which is decentralized. So, what precisely does that imply, and how does it operate?

Cryptocurrency is a new word for most people, so let's write a definition of cryptocurrency. Cryptocurrency is electronic money created with technology that controls its creation and protects transactions while hiding its users ' identities.

Cryptocurrencies are digital cash built to be faster, cheaper, and more secure than money issued by our current government. Instead of trusting a government to create your wealth and banks to store, send, and receive it, users directly transact to each other and save their own money. Without a mediator, people can send money instantly, and transactions are usually very affordable and quick.

In the simplest of words, a cryptocurrency is a digital money. It could be used to buy goods and services. Like traditional money, though, the one big difference here is that most cryptocurrencies ' prices are not fixed-this also makes them an investment opportunity, as investors buy cryptocurrencies at a lower price and sell them when the price increases.

To put it simply, a cryptocurrency is essentially a combination of two words: Crypto+Currency. It is a currency that is encrypted cryptographically.

Cryptocurrencies are digital currencies that can be used to safely transfer money to another person directly, without needing to use third-party intermediaries or trusted parties, such as a bank or Visa, for example, to check that you have sent the money and that the money is not yours anymore. Maybe you want to re-read that sentence slowly. Furthermore, it does it at a fraction of the cost much faster because it reduces unnecessary and expensive transaction fees.

Each user of a cryptocurrency should simultaneously record and check their transactions, and everyone else's purchases to avoid fraud and exploitation. The archives of digital sales are known as a "ledger," and this ledger is open to anyone in particular. Transactions with this public ledger become efficient, permanent, secure, and transparent.

Cryptocurrencies with public records don't require you to trust a bank to hold your money. They don't need that you believe the person with whom you are doing business to pay you. Instead, you can see the money that thousands of people send, receive, verify, and record. This system does not require trust. This unique positive quality is called trust lessness.

Bitcoin was the first to cryptocurrencies.

Below is a list of things each cryptocurrency has to be to call it a cryptocurrency;

1. Digital: Even computers have cryptocurrency. There are no notes and no coins. There are no crypto funds in Fort Knox or at the Bank of England!
2. Decentralized: There is no central computer or server for Cryptocurrencies. They are (typically) distributed across a network of thousands of computers. Systems are called open networks without a central server.

3. Peer-to-peer: Online exchanges of Cryptocurrencies from person to person. Users do not communicate with each other via banks, PayPal, or Facebook. They do deal directly with each other. Banks, Twitter, and PayPal, are all respected third parties.

   Cryptocurrency does not have reliable third parties! Note: They are called trusted third parties because consumers have to trust them to use their services using their personal information. We believe our money in the bank, for example, and we trust Facebook with our holiday photos!

4. Pseudonymous: It means that to own and use cryptocurrencies, you don't need to send any personal information. There are no rules about who owns cryptocurrencies or can use them.

5. Trust less: No trusted third party means users don't have to trust the system to make it work. Consumers are always entirely in control of their money and their expertise.

6. Encrypted: Which user has special codes that stop other users from accessing their information. That is called cryptography, and hacking is almost impossible. It is also from where the crypto part of the definition of crypto comes. Crypt stands for hidden. If cryptography masks knowledge, it is encrypted.

7. Global: Countries have currencies of their own, called fiat currencies. It is difficult to send out fiat currencies around the world. Cryptocurrencies can quickly be sent to anywhere in the world. Cryptocurrencies are non-Border currencies.

A public ledger system called' blockchain' tracks all cryptocurrency transactions. The blockchain technology has several applications, from which one is to record cryptocurrency transactions.

What's Blockchain about?

Blockchain is technology to create permanent, secure digital records that are not dependent on any individual or group. Blockchains may record any details, while Bitcoin transactions were documented in the first example.

Imagine the Blockchain as a documentation book. Each page in that book is a document, and anything can be registered. Blocks are chained one after the other, forming what we know as the Blockchain.

Many of the unrelated individuals and their computers keep multiple blockchain records simultaneously, making it cloud storage on steroids. Immediate changes are seen, and manipulation is extremely difficult/unlikely. This positive quality known to many people is known as "distributed," keeping their copies of the Blockchain.

Many groups create hundreds of blockchains to record all kinds of information, including art, medical records, computer information, and much more.

But if a blockchain isn't distributed among many people, and instead run by one government, company, party, or person, then it's not at all at a blockchain. Such a centralized system is simply a database.

To exclude third parties from their processes, all cryptocurrencies use distributed ledger technology (DLT). DLTs are shared databases that record transaction information. The DLT most used for cryptocurrencies is called the blockchain technology. The first Blockchain was created for Bitcoin by Satoshi Nakamoto.

A blockchain is a database of any transaction ever occurring using a particular cryptocurrency. Data groups called blocks are added one by one to the database and form a very long list. Therefore, a blockchain is a linear blockchain! When blockchain information is added, it cannot be deleted or modified. It lives on the ledger forever and can be seen by everyone.

The entire database is stored on a network of thousands of so-called nodes. You can only add new information to the Blockchain if more than half of the nodes agree that it's valid and correct. This is what is termed consensus. One of the significant differences between crypto-currency and standard banking is the idea of agreement.

Transaction data is stored at a standard bank inside the bank. Bank staff ensures there are no fraudulent transactions. That is known as authentication.

Blockchain is a special kind or subset of so-called distributed ledger ("DLT") technology. DLT is a way to record and share data through multiple data stores (also known as ledgers), each of which has precisely the same data records and is collectively managed and controlled by a centralized computer server network, which is called nodes.

Blockchain is a system that uses the encryption method known as cryptography. It uses (a collection of) unique mathematical algorithms to build and verify a continuously growing data structure–to which data can only be added and from which existing data cannot be removed–that consists of a chain of "transaction blocks" that functions as a distributed ledger. Blockchain is a system with many "facings" in operation. It can view various features and cover a wide range of systems, ranging from being fully open and permission-free to being permitted.

• A person can enter or leave the network at will on a public, permission-free blockchain, without any (central) entity having to (pre-)approve. All it takes to join the network and add transactions to the ledger is a device that has installed the necessary program on. There is no central network and program creator, and all the nodes in the system are distributed identical copies of the ledger. Currently, in circulation, the vast majority of cryptocurrencies are based on permission less blockchains (e.g., Bitcoin, Bitcoin Cash, Litecoin).

• Transaction validators (i.e., nodes) must be pre-selected on a licensed blockchain by a network administrator (which sets the rules for a ledger) to be able to join the network. It helps the identity of the network members, among others, to be easily verified. At the same time, however, it also needs network participants to place trust in a central coordinating body for the selection of reliable network nodes. In general, approved blockchains may be further broken down into two subcategories. On the one side, there are open or publicly available blockchains that can be accessed and viewed by anyone, but where only authorized participants in the network can produce transactions and update the ledger status.

On the other hand, there are authorized blockchains that are closed or "enterprise," where access is restricted, and only the network administrator can produce transactions and change the ledger status. What's important to note is that just like on an encrypted permission less blockchain, transactions on an open permitted blockchain can be validated and executed without trusted third-party intermediation. Many cryptocurrencies, such as Ripple and NEO, use licensed blockchains from the public.

What is Crypto-trading?

The idea is a simple one. You trade one cryptocurrency for another, hoping the coin you are purchasing will increase in value.

This concept is identical to the stock exchange in the real world.

Users need to use a cryptocurrency exchange while trading. This is so you can match buyers and sellers.

This form of trading includes exchanging one cryptocurrency for another, buying and selling coins, and exchanging fiat money for cryptocurrency.

This holds some parallels to foreign exchange (forex), where fiat currencies are traded 24 hours a day from around the globe.

During the last few years, the range of cryptocurrencies has exploded-and estimates suggest that 2,000 exist now.

Many of these coins can be bought only through a significant cryptocurrency such as Bitcoin or Ethereum. Because of this, if you want to contribute to initial coin offerings (ICOs), or use the services of a blockchain company, you'll need to do business.

One drawback to crypto-trading is that without mining coins, you can get involved–a process that takes time, resources, technical know-how, and a lot of computing power.

Crypto-currency markets are decentralized, meaning they are not issued or endorsed by a central authority like a government. Then, they are operating over a computer network. Cryptocurrencies can, however, be purchased and sold through exchanges and stored in' wallets.'

In comparison to traditional currencies, cryptocurrencies function only as a shared ownership ledger, stored on a blockchain. When a user decides to transfer units of cryptocurrency to another user, they send it to the digital wallet of that user. The transaction is not considered final until it is checked through a process called mining and applied to the Blockchain. This is also how new tokens for the cryptocurrency are generally created.

1.2 How a Blockchain works

A blockchain is a shared coded data digital register. This is the transaction background for cryptocurrencies for each unit of the cryptocurrency, which demonstrates how ownership has changed over time. Blockchain operates by storing in' blocks ' transactions, adding new blocks at the front of the chain. Blockchain technology has unique security features that are not compatible with standard computer files.

Network Consensus A blockchain file is always distributed across a network on multiple computers–rather than at a single location–and is generally readable by all within the system. It makes it both transparent and very difficult to modify, with no hacks or human or machine error susceptible to any weak point.

Cryptography Blocks are linked by cryptography–complex mathematics and informatics. Any attempt to alter data interrupts the cryptographic links between blocks, and computers in the network can quickly identify themselves as fraudulent.

In the easiest of ways, a blockchain is a time-stamped collection of permanent data records that is maintained by a network of computers not operated by any single entity. Each of these data blocks (i.e., block) is secured using cryptographic principles (i.e., chain) and connected.

So, what's so unique about it, and why do we say it has capabilities that disrupt the industry?

The blockchain network is without a central authority— it is the very definition of a democratized system. Since it is a public and permanent ledger, the information contained in it is open to all to see. Therefore, by its very nature, everything that is created on the Blockchain is transparent, and all concerned are responsible for their actions.

There is no transaction cost in a blockchain. (Yes, for infrastructure but no transaction costs.) The Blockchain is an easy but ingenious way of fully automated and stable transmission of information from A to B. One party to a transaction initiates the process through a block creation. Thousands of computers check this block, maybe millions, scattered around the net. A chain that is stored on the net is attached to the checked block, creating not just a unique record but an exceptional record with a unique history. Falsifying a single file would mean, in millions of instances, distorting the entire chain. That's almost impossible. Bitcoin uses this money transaction model, but it can be implemented in many other ways.

Think of a railroad company. We buy tickets on the internet or an iPhone. The credit card company is taking a cut to handle the fee. The railway company cannot only save money on credit card processing fees with Blockchain but can also shift the whole ticketing system to the Blockchain. The two parties involved in the transaction are the train company and the passenger. The ticket is a block to be added to a blockchain ticket. Just as a single, independently verifiable, and unfalsifiable record (like Bitcoin) is a monetary transaction on the Blockchain, so may your card be. The final blockchain ticket, by the way, is also a record of all sales for, say, a particular train route, or even the entire train network that includes every ticket ever sold, every journey ever made.

But this is the trick here: It's secure. Not only can the Blockchain pass and store money, but any processes and business models which rely on a small transaction fee may also be replaced

The problems are more evident in the financial world, and the revolutionary changes are imminent. Blockchains will alter the workings of stock exchanges, bundling loans, and contracting insurances. This would remove bank accounts and almost all of the facilities that banks offer. Once the benefits of a stable ledger without transaction fees are widely understood and applied, nearly every financial firm will declare bankruptcy or be forced to make fundamental changes. Indeed, the financial system is based on cutting the money slightly to encourage a transaction. Bankers will become mere counsellors, not money gatekeepers. Stockbrokers won't be able to collect commissions anymore, and the distribution of buy/sell will go out.

Assume a spreadsheet replicated hundreds of times across a computer network. Suppose then that this network is built to update this spreadsheet periodically, and you've got a basic blockchain understanding.

Information collected in a blockchain is available as a shared database and continually reconciled. This is a way to use a network that has advantages. The blockchain database is not stored at any location, which means the records it holds are really public and easily verifiable. A crooked hacker doesn't have a centralized version of this information. Hosted simultaneously by millions of computers, anyone on the internet can access their data.

The reason the Blockchain has gained so much admiration is that:

• A single entity does not own it, therefore it is decentralized

• The data is kept cryptographically within the Blockchain

• The Blockchain cannot be modified so that no one can interfere with the data inside the Blockchain

• The Blockchain is transparent so that you can track the data if you want to.

The network is a set of nodes, which are interconnected. Nodes are individual input-taking computers that perform a task on them and give output. The Blockchain uses a unique sort of peer-to-peer network, which divides its entire workload between participants, all of whom are equally privileged, called peers. There is no longer one central repository, and now there are many peers who are distributed and decentralized.

Consider these quick points in a blockchain as a step-by-step process:

1. A node initiates a transaction by making it first and then signing it digitally with its private key (created by cryptography). In a blockchain, a transaction can represent different actions. Most generally, this is a data structure representing value transfer between users on the blockchain network. Transaction data structure usually consists of some value transfer logic, related rules, addresses to source and destination, and other validation information.

2. Using a flooding protocol, called the Gossip protocol, a transaction is propagated (flooded) to peers who validate the transaction based on present criteria. Usually, it takes more than one node to approve the transaction.

3. Upon confirmation of the transaction, it is included in a chain, which is then propagated to the network. The transaction is deemed verified at this stage.

4. The newly created block is now becoming part of the ledger, and the next block is cryptographically linking itself back to this block. The relation is a pointer to hash. The transaction is getting its second confirmation at this point, and the neighbourhood is getting its first confirmation.

5. Any time a new block is made, transactions are then reconfirmed. In a network.

6. Authorizations usually are required to consider the final transaction.

   Any time a new block is made, transactions are then reconfirmed. In the Bitcoin network, typically, six confirmations are required to consider the final transaction.

1.3 Exploring the Market of cryptocurrency

Cryptocurrency is a disruptive concept used in the current monetary system as an alternative to fiat currency. Entrepreneurs, start-ups, and large as well as small and medium-sized enterprises (SMEs) take an interest in cryptocurrencies and consider it a groundbreaking tool to combat transactional compliances. Because of these reasons, the ecosystem has attracted vast venture funding, alliances, and partnerships among vendors of cryptocurrency solutions to provide end-to-end solutions.

Cryptocurrency is a disruptive concept used in the current monetary system as an alternative to fiat currency. Entrepreneurs, start-ups, and large as well as small and medium-sized enterprises (SMEs) take an interest in cryptocurrencies and consider it a disruptive tool to combat transactional compliances. Because of these reasons, the ecosystem has attracted vast venture funding, alliances, and partnerships among vendors of cryptocurrency solutions to provide end-to-end solutions.

Plenty of people invest in building payment gateways and websites for their currencies. When a customer makes a purchase using a cryptocurrency as payment, the transaction often passes a fixed exchange rate through the payment gateway. It translates immediately to commonly accepted fiat currency so that the merchant can escape the cryptocurrency market instability. Cryptocurrency payment has several advantages, such as improved transactional security, fraud protection, decentralized framework, low fees, customer chargeback protection, and rapid international transfers.

The market for cryptocurrency is categorized by part, size, end-user, and location. It is divided into hardware and software by component. It is divided into FPGA, GPU, ASIC, Wallet, and others within the Hardware category. It is divided into the mining platform and Blockchain under the software section, and coin wallet underneath. It is graded by form into Bitcoin, Ethereum, Ripple (XRP), Litecoin, Dashcoin, etc. It is classified as banking, real estate, and stock market & virtual currency by end-user. It is studied region-wise throughout North America, Europe, Asia-Pacific, and LAMEA.

Intel Corporation, Microsoft Corporation, NVIDIA Corporation, BitFury Group Limited, Alphapoint Corporation, Advanced Micro Devices, Inc., Xilinx Inc., BitGo, Ripple and BTL Group Ltd are some of the major players operating in the sector.

Market capitalization for common shares is a well-known metric but has particular consequences in cryptography. Market capitalization is a calculation of a security's worth. It is typically a ratio of the number of outstanding stock shares by the current stock price. In crypto, it is known as the current price multiplied by the circulating supply of tokens. If a coin has an outstanding 100 tokens and a coin trades for $10, it has a market cap of $1000. There are some 16.6 million bitcoins in existence, and at the time of writing, the price is around $5600. Hence the market cap of Bitcoin is approximately $94 billion.

Traditionally, by financial metrics and ratios, stocks and bonds have been evaluated. Measures such as price-to-earnings ratio, earnings per share, current ratio, earnings growth, and so forth are used for the stock review. Crypto teams do not issue financial statements; however, what metrics do exist is the more critical Market cap offers a quick and easy check on how valuable a cryptocurrency is. The bitcoin sits at nearly $94 billion. Ethereum is the second-largest, at $32bn. Ripple ($10bn, Bitcoin Cash ($5bn), and Litecoin ($3bn) round out top 5.

Just by testing the market caps, you can learn a lot about crypto. First things: Bitcoin is still the big dog in the city. At nearly 55 percent of the total market cap on crypto, the most valuable coin remains far and away, roughly three times as expensive as Ethereum. There's an enormous gap between Bitcoin and Ethereum, but there's also a big gap between Ethereum and Ripple in sixth. Relatively few valuable cryptocurrencies still exist. Only 12 coins have a total $1 billion market cap. It's not unusual to have market caps of under $20 million for leading altcoins. Most of the market cap for crypto remains tied up in Bitcoin and some other big names.

Bitcoin's market cap of $94 billion is massive in a vacuum, but let's put it against some other big names. Bitcoin also jumped along with Goldman Sachs and its market cap of $92 billion. It does have a long way to go, though. JP Morgan, whose CEO Jaime Diamon has bashed Bitcoin publicly, is valued at around $324bn. Facebook amounts to about $500 billion and Apple's $811 billion in leaps forward. So, the brainchild of Satoshi has a long way to go before it seizes the world.

A high or low market cap may reveal a volatility-resistant or vulnerable coin. Consequently, coins with small market caps rock more when big news hits the market, or where "whales" (large buyers) take positions. That's not shocking actually-the crypto markets are among the most competitive the world has ever seen. Yet tokens holders with small market caps are at risk of being overwhelmed by more prominent dealers. If several whales conspire to sell at the same time, a token's price will immediately crash to nothing. For Bitcoin and Ethereum, which have significant market values and are not easily manipulated, that would be much harder.

For another explanation, there is more than a market cap that meets the eye. A market cap is merely a number that reflects the amount and price of circulating coins. It cannot tell who holds those coins, whether it be a whale or a developer. As we have said, a massive token holder can have a significant impact on a coin's price. Several tokens have also taken on flack for developers holding large quantities of coins. When development teams contain large amounts of coins, they can retain control over the token's course, thus promoting a coin's presence with a healthy market cap. Ripple was targeted for this before his latest Bull Run.

This year Bitcoin and Ethereum exploded into mainstream news with massive increases in their respective market caps. They, and Litecoin, the third coin on Coinbase, have all recently seen a boost. Coinbase announced that customers with U.S. bank accounts could make instant purchases which had previously been limited. With this news, all three coins had seen a rise in their respective market caps.

A market cap is both a quick way to gauge the worth of a coin and more than it would seem. A healthy market cap is indicative of a stable coin, but coin holding developers or whales can mislead. Until making an investment decision, always balance market cap with some of the other metrics that we cover.

1.4 What do you need to know about cryptocurrency

Cryptocurrencies, like any currency, can be used to purchase goods and services. Yet cryptocurrencies, unlike other currencies, are digital and use cryptography to provide secure online transactions.

While it is possible to use cryptocurrencies to purchase things, much of the value in these unregulated currencies is to exchange them for income, with speculators often pushing prices skyward.

Cryptocurrencies cater for a variety of reasons to its backers. Here are some of the most sought after:

• Supporters view cryptocurrencies like bitcoin as future currency and are rushing to buy them now, probably before they become more expensive

• Some supporters such as the idea that cryptocurrency eliminates central banks from controlling the money supply because over time these banks tend to reduce the value of money via inflation

• Other supporters, such as the rationale? Just like real currencies, cryptocurrencies do not produce any cash flow, so somebody has to pay more for the money than you do for you to benefit.

That's what investment philosophy is called "the bigger fool." Contrast that to a well-managed business, which increases its value over time by expanding the operation's profitability and cash flow.

There's no doubt they're legal in the U.S., but China has effectively prohibited their use, and mostly whether they're legal depends on each country. Also, be sure to consider how to defend yourself from fraudsters who see cryptocurrencies as an opportunity for investors to bilk on. Purchaser watches out, as always.

If you want to buy a Cryptocurrency at an ICO, read the fine print for this detail in the company's prospectus:

- Who owns the company? A known and identifiable owner is a positive sign.

- Are there any other big investors that invest in it? If other well-known investors want a slice of the currency, it is a good sign.

- Will you own a corporate stake, or just money or tokens? That is an important distinction. Owning a share means you are eligible to participate in its profits (you are an owner), whereas buying tokens means you have the right to use them, like chips in a casino.

- Is the currency already created, or does the organization try to raise money for its development?

The further along with the product, the less risky it is. Combing through a prospectus can take a lot of work; the more detail it has, the better your chances it is legitimate. But even credibility doesn't mean success for currency. That is an entirely separate question, and that requires a great deal of market expertise.

But beyond those issues, just possessing cryptocurrency exposes you to the risk of theft, as hackers try to penetrate the networks of computers that protect your properties. One high profile exchange declared bankruptcy in 2014 after hackers in bitcoins stole hundreds of millions of dollars. These are not typical risks of investing in major U.S. exchanges in stocks and funds.

Several vendors are embracing cryptocurrencies. For example, Microsoft would allow you to add Bitcoin to your online account using your digital wallet. And there's a rising number of things you can buy using cryptocurrencies, including all from fine art to real estate. The adoption of cryptocurrency payments has, in many cases, was more of a marketing move than financially realistic, but it can give more stability to the cryptocurrency tokens.

On the upside, you should be aware that most outlets accepting cryptocurrencies have put significant limitations and restrictions on it. Firstly, most accept only the leading cryptocurrencies, Bitcoin, and Ethereum. Second, you may not be in a position to use the credit for any operation. For instance, Microsoft will let you use Bitcoin to buy games, movies, and software in Windows and Xbox stores — but you can't purchase gift cards with it in the online store.

Any hidden charges?

Of course, it is! Many independent exchanges and companies that will buy and sell cryptocurrencies will charge you some fee for the service. Then, like real stock traders, each time you buy or sell a currency, they get you to come and go. The fees usually represent a percentage of the total deposit or payment. Even if you still have to pay 1.5% of the overall, however, this is much less than some other conventional services.

Is it safe?

That hinges on your perspective. It's true that cryptocurrencies using blockchain technology ensure transactions are correctly recorded and make hacking very difficult. Blockchain software is a decentralized ledger that is not managed by any single person or institution because all transactions are registered through multiple nodes, providing transparency and making it extremely difficult for any user to manipulate.

Is that different than other payment services online?

In a nutshell, no. The fundamental problem with all cryptocurrencies is their predictable value fluctuation. So, while you're holding onto any specific digital currency, you may lose (or gain) money until you use it to buy or unload something. Modern money (what crypto supporters call "fiat" currency) appears to be more robust, as it is backed by governments and a much more extensive global trading market network.

But before you start plunging into the craze of cryptocurrency, here are some facts you should remember.

1. Digital currencies are highly unpredictable
2. Unlike the U.S. dollars in your wallet or any other money around the world, digital currencies are not backed up by a central bank or government.
3. There are more than 2,000 (but bitcoin is king) cryptocurrencies.
4. Blockchain lies where is the real value.
5. "Miners" play a critical role, but to account for new transactions and transfers, cryptocurrency transactions need to be checked, and the Blockchain periodically extended. The job falls to a group of people called cryptocurrency miners.
6. Decentralization is key. The fact that it's decentralized is what makes blockchain technology so enticing.
7. The entry barrier is relatively low. It should also be noted that while blockchain technology could change the landscape for the financial services industry, there is virtually no entry barrier. If you have time, resources, and a coding team, you can theoretically write Blockchain and put a cryptocurrency onto the market.
8. Cryptocurrencies in several countries are forbidden. Of course, cryptocurrencies may be the hottest thing since sliced bread, but they are not approved anywhere. Thanks to their unregulated and decentralized nature, some countries have opted to prohibit the use and exchange of digital currencies outright.

9. Many citizens still have limited knowledge of what are or legal 16 cryptocurrencies.

Tax department still wants it to be fair share:

Last but not least, don't presume that you're getting a free ride on any money you're pocketing just because cryptocurrencies are unregulated. The Internal Revenue Service (IRS) also wants you to pay tax on your income from cryptocurrencies, and to make sure that happens, and it is doing everything in its power.

Chapter 2: Classification of Cryptocurrencies

There was a time when one hand could be counting the number and forms of cryptocurrency. That is no longer feasible today. The crypto-market expanded grew and grew a little more!

Currently, there are nearly 2,000 different coins and tokens in the cryptocurrency world, each having their applications and solving a specific problem.

Bitcoin has traditionally been the king of the mountain when it comes to cryptocurrencies, due to its position as the founder and first-mover appeal of the young industry. The first cryptocurrency is still the most popular one on the market a decade later.

But there are hundreds of other digital currencies out there, apart from the bitcoin. These are known as "altcoins," or alternatives to bitcoin; for example, to name a few, ether, ripple, zcash, monero, and dash.

Altcoins can vary in a variety of ways from Bitcoin.

The third dominant form of cryptocurrency is a token— the same sort we just spoke about! They are peculiar in their lack of blockchain compared to the other two significant types of crypto-currency.

Tokens always have a premium to sell for, which is why some people buy them.

Let's further explore each of these in-depth.

2.1 What is a Bitcoin

Bitcoin was developed by the pseudonym Satoshi Nakamoto, an anonymous group or individual. Bitcoin is Software Open Source.

Bitcoin is an electronic type of cash, a crypto-currency. It is a decentralized digital currency that can be sent to the peer-to-peer Bitcoin blockchain network from the user to the consumer without the need for intermediaries without a central bank or a single admin.

Bitcoin founders wanted to take responsibility for the seller, remove the middleman, cancel interest charges, and make transactions open, hack corruption, and slash fees. They have created a decentralized system where you can control your funds and know what was going on there.

Bitcoin is not a fiat currency and has no government ties. This is a cryptocurrency and can be used either for transaction or investment purposes. Most mainstream companies accept Bitcoin as payment, and even some governments do.

Bitcoin is either virtual currency or a technology guide at its purest. Transactions can be made by checking, wiring, or cash. You can also use Bitcoin (or BTC) to pass your signature to the recipient, which is a long line of encoded security code with 16 distinct symbols. The buyer decodes the system to get your crypto-currency with his smartphone. Cryptocurrency is a digital information exchange that lets you buy or sell goods and services. By operating on a peer-to-peer computer network similar to Skype or BitTorrent, a file-sharing system, the transaction achieves its protection and trust.

Before getting into the technical details, Bitcoin operates on a massive public ledger, also called a blockchain, where all verified transactions are included as so-called' blocks.' As each block passes into the system, it is distributed for confirmation to the peer-to-peer user computer network. Both consumers are thus aware of each transaction, which avoids cheating and double-spending, where somebody spends twice the same currency. The method also helps users of the blockchain confide in the program.

The price to purchase a bitcoin— the first and most popular digital currency in the world— broke $8,000 in May, after trade as low as $3,237 in Dec. The recent highs are encouraging to enthusiasts for cryptocurrency, but still a long way from the meteoric rise of Bitcoin in 2017, when its price approached $20,000.

When prices rise, so does the interest of the public in buying bitcoin.

"What might be required is an electronic payment system based on cryptographic evidence rather than confidence, enabling any two willing parties to trade directly with each other without the need for a trusted third party, "wrote Satoshi Nakamoto — the enigmatic bitcoin creator's alias, which remains unknown — in a white paper introducing open source technology.

Bitcoin (the "BTC" trading symbol, though "XBT" is also used) is a computer file stored on a computer or smartphone in a digital wallet. To grasp how Bitcoin works, few words and a little description help to understand:

• Blockchain: Bitcoin is propelled by the open-source code referred to as the blockchain, which generates a shared public ledger. -the transaction is a "bar" that is "chained" to the system, making -transactions a permanent record. Blockchain technology is at the core of over 2,200 cryptocurrencies that have emerged in the wake of bitcoin.

• Private and public keys: A Bitcoin wallet contains a public key and a private key, which work together to enable the owner to initiate and sign transactions digitally, providing proof of authorization.

• Bitcoin miners: Miners— or peer-to-peer platform members — then confirm the purchase independently using high-speed computers, typically within 10 to 20 minutes. Miners get paid for their efforts in bitcoin.

Bitcoin value follows the law of supply and demand — and there is a lot of volatility in the price of the cryptocurrency, as demand waxes and wanes.

The best thing about Bitcoin is that it is decentralized, meaning you can settle international deals with exchange rates and additional charges without messing around. Bitcoin is free of interference and manipulation by the government, so there is no Federal Reserve System for hiking interest rates. It's transparent too, so you know what's going on with your money. You can start accepting bitcoins immediately, without spending money and energy in information like setting up a merchant account or buying equipment for processing credit cards. Bitcoins can't be stolen, nor can the customer ask for a refund.

The users call Bitcoin "Money 2.0" or that Bill Gates called it "a digital tour de force" is a small wonder. You can't stop something like Bitcoin. "It will be all over the place, and the world will have to re-adjust". John McAfee, McAfee's founder.

It's kind of like an online cash version. This can be used to buy goods and services, but Bitcoin is still not accepted by many shops, and some countries have banned it altogether.

Digital Bitcoins are a phenomenon you see in pictures. Without the secret codes imprinted within them, they would be worthless.

Every Bitcoin is a computer file installed on your smartphone or computer in a' digital wallet' app.

Bitcoins may be sent to your digital wallet (or part of one), and you can send Bitcoins to others.

Every single transaction is registered in a blockchain-called public list.

It allows tracing the past of Bitcoins to discourage people from spending coins that they don't own, making copies or undoing transactions.

There are three main ways that people have Bitcoins.
Bitcoins can be bought using the' real' money.
Selling stuff and letting people pay you with Bitcoins.
Or you can use a computer to create them.

There are many other things besides money that we find essential, like gold and diamonds. The Aztecs made money out of cocoa beans!

Bitcoins are worthwhile because people are willing to trade them for real goods and services, and even for cash.

People can spend their Bitcoins very anonymously too. Although all transactions are registered, unless you told them, nobody would know which' account number' was yours.

That transaction is documented publicly, so copying Bitcoins, making fake ones, or wasting ones you don't own is very difficult.

You can lose your Bitcoin wallet or delete your Bitcoins, and lose them forever. There were also website robberies that let you store your Bitcoins remotely.

Over the years since it was created in 2009, the value of Bitcoins has gone up and down, and some people don't think it's safe to turn your' real' money into Bitcoins.

Bitcoin has completely changed the world's economy and financial systems over the last 11 years. That said, this is merely the beginning. The Bitcoin movement has yet to go several miles. Seeing where we're going to go from here will be super exciting.

2.2 What are ALT coins and Tokens

Bitcoin's emergence has precipitated the proliferation of a lush and more complex ecosystem of other coins and tokens, which are often regarded as cryptocurrencies in general, even though most of them are not described as a "currency."

Please note that all coins or tokens are classified as cryptocurrencies, even though most of the coins do not act like a currency or exchange medium.

The most common Cryptocurrencies categorization is

1. Alternative Coins in Cryptocurrency (Altcoins)

2.Tokens Often, people use the term "coin" to refer to what others call "tokens" and "cash" to mean what others call "coins."

Many people will use either name to refer to all of the currently available digital assets.

There are substantial differences between crypto coins and crypto tokens, though, so you must know what they are!

Alternative coins are called altcoins or only "coins." Also, they are used interchangeably. Altcoins refers simply to the coins that are an alternative to Bitcoin. Many altcoins are a variant (fork) of Bitcoin, developed using the open-sourced, initial protocol of Bitcoin with modifications in its underlying codes, thereby conceiving an utterly new coin with a specific set of features.

Other altcoins aren't derived from the open-source protocol of Bitcoin. Instead, they developed their Blockchain and contract supporting their native currency. Ethereum, Ripple, Omni, Nxt, Waves, and Counterparty are examples of such coins.

One common feature of all altcoins is that they each have a separate ledger where their native coins are transacted in.

Usually, digital coins are used in the same way as a real-life coin is - as currency. Just like the coins in your pocket or piggy bank, you might think of coins like Bitcoin, Litecoin, and Monero. Sometimes, they serve no purpose other than being used as capital.

Such "cash only" coins are used:

- Using them to transfer money (you can give and receive interest)

- As a store of value (you can save them and later change them to something useful)

- As an account unit (You can price goods or services therein) Let's use Bitcoin as an example to ensure you understand the above.

- The BTC can be used to pay for products and services throughout the internet and in many places in the real world.

- You can store it for a long time, and nothing happens. You can then later swap it for something of equal value.

- The goods you buy can also be priced in BTC.

There's no other use for Bitcoin other than those commercial applications. It can't be staked to receive more Bitcoins, and it doesn't have to be used to run any program. It's used as money and all of that.

Tokens reflect a particular asset or utility, which typically sits on top of another blockchain. Tokens can represent virtually any fungible and tradable assets, from commodities to loyalty points to even other cryptocurrencies.

Tokens are often termed digital coins. This doesn't seem right, though. There is one big difference!

On current blockchains, tokens are developed. The most common blockchain token platform is Ethereum, thanks to the creation and facilitation of smart contracts. On the Ethereum platform, tokens are known as ERC-20 tokens.

The majority of tokens are for use with decentralized applications, or dApps. When developers create their token, they can decide how many units they want to make and where when they are created, these new tokens will be sent to. They'll pay some of the native cryptocurrency for the Blockchain on which they're building the token right now.

Once developed, tokens are often used to enable the application features to which they were intended.

Musicoin, for example, is a token that allows users to access the various Musicoin platform features. This might be to watch a music video or download a song.

Binance (the exchange) has its token, as well. When BNB (Binance token) users trade, their fees are 50 percent lower.

Some tokens are created for a wholly different purpose: to represent something physical. Let's say you wanted a smart contract for selling your house. You can't put your home physically into the smart contract, can you? No. No.

So, you can instead use a token that reflects your home.

Tokens are assets that act even as a method of payment but through internal token passing within the project concerned, and they carry a value!

A token holder has the right to take part in the event concerned, but a coin holder may not get the advantage.

It's a much easier process to create tokens because you don't have to adjust the codes of a given protocol or build a blockchain from scratch. The most you can do is to follow a standard blockchain template–like on the Ethereum or Waves platform–that allows you to create your tokens. This functionality of creating your tokens is made possible by using smart contracts, programmable, self-executing computer codes that don't need any third parties to operate. It's super cool, yeah!

To conclude, the main difference between altcoins and tokens lies in their structure; altcoins are separate currencies with their different Blockchain, while tokens operate on top of a blockchain that makes decentralized applications more comfortable to create.

Digital coins hold value and refer to it as' market cap.' This rate changes as per demand; more demand or circulation means more value, and the investment gains its upper hand with more value! Like the Bitcoin boom, investors may earn high returns, and use it as a method of payment. The payment platform will endorse the digital currency payment method as well, just in case you are not conscious! That is digital money, let's talk briefly now about tokens.

Let's illustrate tokens with a simple use case if you accept tokens from a team saying you're a well-known direct selling company's product distributor, and they're paying you in terms of tokens rather than fiat currency. Everything you need to do here is that the tokens have a value on a given project but not outside that program. Make sure they have a deal with any of the popular exchanges like Binance, Bitfinex, etc. so you can exchange it for real money later on, or else you might have to prefer fiat currency to pay!

Such token offering companies must register on the exchanges even if you have issued many such tokens, in short, a token must hold real value and serve as a guaranteed asset for later use of such exchange platforms to castrate them.

FYI, coin tokens may be purchased but not vice versa. Coins, coins, etc. are usually based on cryptocurrencies, and this is the main reason why they should be used as synonyms.

2.3 Bitcoin and beyond: the 10 cryptocurrencies with the highest market capitalization

Below are some of the digital currencies other than bitcoin's most popular. Last, however, a caveat: a list like this cannot be completely exhaustive. One explanation for this is that as of January 2020, there are more than 2,000 cryptocurrencies, and many of those tokens and coins enjoy immense popularity among a devoted (if low, in some cases) group of backers and investors.

Please note that, given the continually changing market cap, values that vary from those expressed at the time of publication

1 Bitcoin ($156.52 trillion): Bitcoin became the first cryptocurrency after its launch in 2009 and remained at the forefront of the market ever since. Virtually, Bitcoin eliminated the "middleman" who managed the currency and replaced it with advanced blockchain. About three-fourths of all Bitcoin has been mined already–meaning its value should be moving forward more predictably.

2. Ethereum: ($17.50 trillion) Launching much later than the top dog, Bitcoin, in 2015, Ethereum joined the crypto-currency market.

Whereas Bitcoin provides digital currency peer-to-peer, Ethereum offers smart-contract applications (the user may set specific conditions for activating a transaction). Ethereum has a wide variety of uses that cater to clients looking to do more than financial transactions.

3. Ripple's XRP: ($9.80 trillion) Ripple is a cryptocurrency that was never actually meant to be a cash alternative and is used mostly by corporate institutions rather than individuals. It only takes a few seconds to transfer Ripple coins from one wallet to another; however, it is a much more centralized operation compared to competitors, as Ripple Labs manages XRP's supply.

4. Bitcoin Cash: ($5.76 trillion) Bitcoin Cash, also known as Bcash, is a spinoff Bitcoin created in 2017 by Bitcoin miners and developers. Primarily, the Bitcoin blockchain was split where one cryptocurrency remained as the original Bitcoin, and the other emerged as Bitcoin Cash. Bitcoin Cash has lower transfer fees than Bitcoin and quicker transfer time-that's why it was popular among investors.

5. Bitcoin SV ($5.51 billion): Bitcoin Satoshi Vision (Bitcoin SV) is one of the crypto market's newest players and has ridden rival Bitcoin Cash coattails until recently. Bitcoin SV originated from a split in Bitcoin Cash's network, as BSV developers wanted to restore the initial Bitcoin protocol instead of moving under the Bitcoin Cash blockchain. Block size limits are the critical difference between Bitcoin, Bitcoin Cash, and Bitcoin SV. Bitcoin Cash boosted the size limit of the block to 32 MB, and Bitcoin SV quadrupled the limit to 128 MB.

6.Tether ($4.11 trillion): It differs from Bitcoin in that it's a stable coin–meaning it's backed by a reserve statement and designed to offer price stability worth $1.

It was launched in 2014 to facilitate the digital use of fiat currencies (Canadian Dollar, Indian Rupee, European Union Euro) and is the first platform enabled by blockchain to facilitate the digital use of traditional money.

7. Litecoin ($3.57 trillion): In 2011, Bitcoin was divided into two by a hard fork: producing Bitcoin and Litecoin. Key factors separating Litecoin from Bitcoin are the speed of transactions and block reward per day. The transaction time for Litecoin is about four times faster than that of Bitcoin and has 25 block rewards per transaction compared to 12.5 for Bitcoin.

8. EOS ($3.42 trillion): EOS released in 2017, and while other cryptocurrencies are intended for peer-to-peer transactions, The EOS coins are designed for use within the EOS network – similar to the Ethereum framework. The smart contract platform EOS.IO is intended to run millions of transactions per second without feeds and is suitable for developers looking to build their applications or smart contracts.

9. Binance Coin ($2.62 trillion): Binance is a global cryptocurrency exchange service for over 100 cryptocurrencies, meaning it is intended to link buyers to trading sellers. As of 2019, it has partnered with Israeli payment processor Simplex to facilitate debit and credit card transactions of Bitcoin, Ethereum, Litecoin and Ripple's XRP. Binance also makes deposits and withdrawals free to consumers.

10. Monero ($1.12 billion): While Monero's mining process is much slower than Bitcoin's rival, and the algorithm is not much different from ordinary computers, which helps it to meet a more extensive user base.

One of the critical points which bring Monero to the list of top cryptocurrencies is that its security and privacy capabilities render transactions anonymous and untraceable;

Monero uses cryptography to secure the transmitting addresses, as well as the sums transacted.

Chapter 3: Operating Cryptocurrency

Bitcoin has altered the way people think of money. There have been hundreds of other cryptocurrencies created since then, and they all want to change the world!

Establishing a Cryptocurrencies definition is not an easy task. Cryptocurrencies, like blockchain, has become a "buzzword" to refer to a wide range of technological developments using a technique better known as cryptography. Cryptography is the technique of protecting information by transforming it (i.e., encrypting it) into an unreadable format, which can only be deciphered (or decrypted) by someone who has a secret key. Cryptocurrencies, like Bitcoin, are secured using this strategy, using an innovative network of encrypted public and private keys.

Operating cryptocurrency involves a lot of steps and also consists of a lot of players, such as trading positions, miners, wallet service providers, and more.

3.1 Role of Users, Miners, Exchanges, Trading Platforms, Wallet providers, Coin Inventors, and Coin offerors

The market for cryptocurrencies is a new playing field where different actors each play a specific role. To shed some more light on how the market works, and without trying to be exhaustive, we will describe the key players and their positions further below.

Cryptocurrency users: The "cryptocurrency user" is a first and significant player. A cryptocurrency consumer is a natural person or legal entity who obtains coins to use them for:

(i) I buying real or virtual goods or services (from a set of specific merchants78),

(ii) making P2P payments, or

(iii) keeping them for investment purposes (i.e., in a thoughtful manner).

Without trying to be exhaustive, a cryptocurrency consumer may acquire his coins in several ways.

• First, he can buy his coins on a cryptocurrency exchange using fiat money or another cryptocurrency;

• Second, he can buy his coins directly from another cryptocurrency user (i.e., via a trading platform–this type of exchange is often referred to as a "P2P Exchange");

Miners: A second player is the "miner," who is interested in the validation of blockchain transactions by solving a "cryptographic puzzle." As described above, the mining process relates to cryptocurrencies, which are based on a system of PoW consensus. By using computing power to verify transactions, a miner supports the network and is compensated with freshly mined coins (i.e., through an automatically decentralized new issue).

Miners can be consumers of cryptocurrency, or, more generally, parties that have done a new mining coin business to sell them for fiat currency (such as US dollar or Euro) or other cryptocurrencies. Many miners combine to bundle computing power in so-called mine pools. The risks associated with the so-called "mining companies" seem to be overlooked at the moment. Below, we'll expand on that more.

Cryptocurrency exchanges: The so-called "cryptocurrency exchanges" are the third group of key players. Cryptocurrency exchanges are individuals or organizations that provide cryptocurrency users exchange services, usually against payment of a specified fee (i.e., a commission). They allow users of the cryptocurrency to sell their fiat currency coins or buy new fiat currency coins. They usually function as both a stock exchange office and a form of the exchange office.

Examples of well-known cryptocurrency exchanges include Bitfinex, HitBTC, Kraken, and Coinbase GDAX. It is important to note that some exchanges are pure cryptocurrency exchanges, meaning they only accept payments in other cryptocurrencies, generally, Bitcoin (e.g., Binance).

In contrast, others accept payments in fiat currencies such as US dollars or Euro (e.g., Coinbase). Furthermore, many cryptocurrency exchanges only require their users to purchase a limited set of coins. It should also be remembered that many cryptocurrency exchanges (i.e., standard as well as pure cryptocurrency exchanges) act as wallet custodian providers (e.g., Bitfinex).

In general, cryptocurrency exchanges offer a wide range of payment options for their customers, such as wire transfers, PayPal transfers, credit cards, and other coins. Many cryptocurrency exchanges also provide cryptocurrency market statistics (such as trading volumes and prices of exchanged coins) and offer conversion services to merchants that accept payments in cryptocurrencies.

Trading platforms: In parallel to exchanges for cryptocurrencies, so-called "trading platforms" still play an essential role in cryptocurrencies trade (and, most notably, allow users of cryptocurrencies to purchase cash coins). Trading platforms are marketplaces that bring together different users of cryptocurrency who are either interested in buying or selling cryptocurrencies, providing them with a forum where they can trade directly with each other (i.e., an "eBay" for cryptocurrency). Often, trading platforms are called "P2P exchanges" or "decentralized exchanges." They differ in several ways from the crypto-currency exchanges. Next, they don't buy or sell the coins themselves.

Furthermore, they are not run by an agency or corporation that regulates and manages all trades but is controlled solely by software (i.e., no central point of authority exists).

Trading platforms connect a buyer to a seller, allowing them to execute a sale, online, or even in-person locally (i.e., a face-to-face transaction, often carried out in cash). A typical example of a Bitcoins trading platform is LocalBitcoins.

Wallet providers: The so-called "wallet providers" are another community of critical players. Wallet providers are those organizations that provide digital wallets or e-wallets to cryptocurrency users that are used to hold, store, and transfer coins. Or put it, a wallet houses the cryptographic keys of a crypto-currency customer.

Usually, a wallet provider converts the transaction history of a cryptocurrency user into an easily readable format, which looks remarkably like a traditional bank account.

There are several types of wallet providers:

• Blockchain wallet providers who provide unique blockchain solutions for cryptocurrency users to privately store their cryptographic keys (e.g., Ledger Wallet);

• Software wallet providers that offer software applications to cryptocurrency users, allow them to access the network, send and receive coins, and save their crypt locally.

Coin inventors: There are those groups, also known as "coin inventors." Coin inventors are individuals or organizations that created a cryptocurrency's technological foundations and laid down the first rules for its use. Its identity is sometimes known (e.g., Ripple, Litecoin, Cardano), but they remain unidentified (e.g., Bitcoin, Monero) ever so often. Others remain active in maintaining and improving the code and the underlying algorithm of the cryptocurrency (in theory without the control of the administrator), while others disappear (e.g., Bitcoin).

Coin offerors: The "coin offerors" are a final category of key players to identify. Coin offerors are individuals or organizations selling coins to cryptocurrency users upon initial release of the coin, either against payment (i.e., by crowd-sale) or at no charge (i.e., under a particular (sign-up) system (e.g., Stellar–see below)), usually to finance more production of the coin or to raise its initial popularity. The coins provided to cryptocurrency users by these coin offerors are produced or mined before the official release of the coin/coin's creation.

Coins distributed this way are either partially pre-mined pre-created (i.e., users of cryptocurrency may still produce more coins after release), or they are pre-mined pre-created in full. The coin offeror typically holds a large portion of the coins in the latter case (for example, this is the case with Stellar). Please take note of this that not all coins have an identifiable offeror of coins, nor are altcoins pre-mined, or are pre-created for their full supply. A coin offeror may be the same person as the maker of the coin, or another entity or organization.

3.2 What is cryptocurrency mining

Cryptocurrency mining may sound like something you're doing with a shovel and a hard hat, but it's more like accounting. Miners are nodes that perform a particular task allowing transactions.

It is the way cryptocurrency networks like Bitcoin check new transactions and validate new ones. This avoids double-spending, as banks do, without having to trust centralized accounting. Crypto-currency blockchains are not secured by people or trust. Computer-led math protects us!

"Mining" refers to a step by which two things happen: Crypto-currency transactions are verified, and new crypto-currency units are created. Active mining requires powerful hardware as well as software.

When it comes to testing, a single computer is not powerful enough to mine cryptocurrencies profitably, because you would run your power bill. Miners often join pools to increase collective computing power to address this, allocating mineral profits to participants. Mining companies compete to check pending transactions and make profits, exploiting advanced hardware, and low-cost electricity. This rivalry helps to ensure that transactions are essential.

Cryptocurrency mining, or crypto mining, is a method in which transactions are checked and applied to the digital blockchain ledger for various forms of cryptocurrency. It is also known as crypto-coin mining, altcoin-mining, or Bitcoin-mining (for cryptocurrency's most popular style, bitcoin), cryptocurrency mining has developed both as a subject and as operation as cryptocurrency use itself has grown exponentially in recent years.

Every time a cryptocurrency transaction is made, it is the duty of a cryptocurrency miner to ensure the validity of the information and update the blockchain with the transaction. The method of mining itself involves interacting with other crypto-miners to overcome complicated mathematical problems associated with cryptographic hash functions associated with a block containing the transaction data.

The very first cryptocurrency miner to unlock the code is credited with the authorization of the transaction, and the cryptominers earn small amounts of their cryptocurrency in return for the service provided. A cryptocurrency miner, therefore, needs a computer with advanced hardware to be competitive with other crypto miners.

Crypto-monetary mining involves two features, namely: introducing blockchain transactions (securing and verifying) and also releasing new currency. Individual blocks inserted by miners should be issued with proof of work or PoW.

Mining needs a computer and a unique program that lets miners engage in solving complicated mathematical problems with their peers. This would require a massive amount of computer resources. In regular intervals, miners will try to solve a block using cryptographic hash functions that have the transaction data.

A hash value is a fixed-length numeric value that uniquely identifies the data. Miners use their machine to zero in on a less than target hash value, and whoever unlocks it first, would be known as the one who mined the block and is eligible for a reward.

The reward for a block being mined now is 12.5 bitcoins (it can differ)

Previously only lovers of cryptography worked as miners. Nevertheless, as cryptocurrencies are increasing in popularity and value, mining is now considered a lucrative sector. Consequently, several individuals and companies have begun investing in warehouses and hardware.

Bitcoin miners also started joining open pools as companies jumped into the fray, unable to compete, sharing resources to compete efficiently.

3.3 Who are the key players

Despite the bearish cryptocurrency climate in 2019, blockchain ventures and influencers in cryptocurrency seem to support the technology with brazen developments and positive expectations for the future.

While secure funding for blockchain may slip away for new start-ups, 2019's top 100 crypto characters show that the 2019 crypto space emphasis tends to lean more towards pushing mass adoption and incorporating blockchain into established enterprise infrastructure.

The top 10 key players in the Crypto world discussed below are:

1. CZ Binance Changpeng Zhao, who goes by CZ, is the founder and CEO of Binance, a cryptocurrency exchange which is just under 180 days became the largest on the planet. The Chinese-Canadian coder cut his teeth designing high-frequency trading networks for flash boys on Wall Street.

2. Jihan Wu is co-founder and chairman of Bitmain Technologies, a Chinese mining-chip company. Bitmain was founded in 2013 and is China's most significant cryptocurrency mining-chip company; it specializes in the selling of ASIC-chip miners.

3. Since 2015, Jack Dorsey Tattooed entrepreneur Jack Dorsey has been the CEO of Twitter, a social media company, and Square, a small business payment firm. Dorsey co-founded Twitter with Ev Williams, Biz Stone and Noah Glass in 2006, and remained CEO until 2008. He was back in 2015.

4. David Marcus the man spearheading Facebook's blockchain effort, David Marcus, has lately got a tremendous amount of spotlight. Libra's rapid growth has dominated the reporting of other crypto-related trends, as it became clear that the inroad of the social media giant into the field of digital assets would have the most severe consequences for both the blockchain industry and the global financial system in general.

5. Brian Armstrong. He is Coinbase's co-founder, an open financial system, and the world's biggest digital currency trading exchange. He graduated from Rice University with a bachelor's degree in computer science, then earned a second bachelor's degree in economics, and eventually a master's degree in computer science. He was also portrayed in the 2014

film "The Rise and Rise of Bitcoin." He may be the single most responsible person to bring cryptocurrencies into the world.

6. Vitalik Howevererin. He is the inventor and creator of Ethereum, a technology based on blockchain, which serves as a platform for decentralized applications. Many non-Ether cryptocurrencies currently reside on the Ethereum blockchain. The crypto-currency, Ether, grew in income and popularity in 2017 and doubled the market value of the company to over $40 billion. He also writes and publishes for Bitcoin Magazine. Buterin is also a committed philanthropist who has donated millions to non-profits and other organizations in Ether.

7. Brad Garlinghouse, He has worked in several well-known tech legacy firms such as AOL, Yahoo, Flickr, and others. Yet his current role is Ripple's CEO, the 2017 highest-performing cryptocurrency. Ripple acts as a network designed for banks to transfer currencies and can quickly and securely finalize international transactions.

8. Charlie Lee. Born in the Ivory Coast, he is considered to be the founder of the accessible Litecoin business and has also served for some time as Coinbase's Engineering Manager. He also manages to find time to focus on other coin-specific projects at Litecoin now again full time. He had worked in engineering positions at Google and Guidewire Software before joining the crypto-currency environment. In reaction to his criticism of the Bitcoin and other revolutionary currency's inherent flaws, perhaps his most significant contribution to crypto-currency, Litecoin, was developed. He built Litecoin to be cheaper, have more coin supply, and use a script-based hashing protocol to make it extremely popular.

9. Roger V. By becoming the first investor in cryptocurrency companies such as Bitcoin.com, Most Trusted Crypto Group, Z. cash, etc., he is considered one of the masterminds behind the growth of cryptocurrencies. Today, he is a frequent speaker at worldwide cryptocurrency conferences. He firmly

believes cryptocurrency is the secret to promoting true economic independence. Considered a bit of a wicked spirit, following his release from prison on a charge of trafficking explosives, he travelled to Japan. He then renounced his US citizenship after securing a passport for Saint Kitts and Nevis. He considers himself an anarchist, an anarcho-capitalist, a champion of peace, and a strong proponent of individualism and voluntarism.

10. John McAfee This ever-active technologist is most famous for pioneering the first anti-virus software on the mass market. Recently, however, he has adopted a liking for the cryptocurrency industry. As such, McAfee holds considerable authority-as he is a physical space veteran.

Chapter 4: Cryptocurrency Trading and Investing

In recent years, cryptocurrencies have been pretty much a topic of intense debate. How many times have we heard stories of people becoming millionaires overnight and, at the same time, stories of people losing hundreds of thousands of dollars in hopes of making a quick buck?

In the cryptocurrency market, the words ' investing' and' trading' have often been used interchangeably. Nonetheless, the two concepts very profoundly that are vital for you to recognize and comply with your financial goals.

There are several ways the Cryptocurrency market can generate wealth for anyone. You can either be a:

a) Miner

B) Investor

C) Trader

Investing is a long-term thing that speaks to basics and long-term trends and is not that concerned with short-term price trends, and trading is a small thing that speaks to technology trends and concerns short-term price trends.

Anyone can combine investment and trading, but the two should not be confused. The existing crypto-currency markets are traders' markets, so those looking to invest will do well over time to carefully construct positions to prevent price fluctuations.

All investing and trading require patience and control over one's emotions, and both can be challenging, but it can be rewarding to get good at either.

A cryptocurrency's value can change very quickly, but with time one can see that the transaction volume has risen while the volatility has continued to drop. It remains to be seen whether the pattern will continue. It's essential to keep in mind the risk of a significant price correction. It is up to each trader and investor to weigh the considerable potential of cryptocurrencies on their own with the dangers that these currencies still face.

4.1 What is the value of cryptocurrencies, how are prices determined, and what could Bitcoin be worth in the future

For the Internet,' HTTP' is a protocol specifying how information is transmitted over the Internet. On the back of those protocols, an application such as Facebook and Google was built by programmers. Although these protocols generated a tremendous value, most of the cost was captured by the applications built on top of the Internet. It means the people who built HTTP weren't making money and are relatively unknown. Nevertheless, Facebook and Google founders have become billionaires and are well-known businessmen.

For Bitcoin, and a platform like Ethereum, the value is created by the actual network itself. Token holders are the ones who'll benefit. Those buildings and investing in the blockchain protocol layer will capture the value because of the financial incentives (tokens) that are part of the design of the network.

Network participants (users, developers, investors, etc.) are encouraged to expand the blockchain network because the tokens will be worth more as the system grows.

In general, the value of a cryptocurrency is derived from its usefulness, use case, and, eventually, demand, among other factors. Learning this will help you make good choices about which crypto-currency coins you trade and invest in.

As with most goods and services, the economic value of cryptocurrencies derives from supply and demand. Quantity refers to how much is available— like the number of Bitcoins available to buy at any time. Demand refers to the desire of individuals to own it— as in how many people would like to buy Bitcoin and how much they want it. A crypto-monetary value will always be a combination of both variables.

There are other value types, as well. There's the interest you get from using a crypto-currency, for example. Most people love to spend or donate crypto because it gives them a sense of pride in helping an exciting new financial system. Likewise, some people enjoy shopping with Bitcoin because they like its low fees and want to inspire businesses to take it on.

In general, the value of a cryptocurrency is derived from its usefulness, use case, and, eventually, demand, among other factors.

Learning this will help you make good choices about which crypto-currency coins you trade and invest in.

Today the value of crypto-currency comes from two sources:

1. People are expecting the cost to go up, and they buy it as an investment, so its value is rising. If expectations shift, the value may crash, then recover, etc.
2. Users need the cryptocurrency so that they can use it. The value goes up, and even if it falls, it remains significant. If the value goes down, it gets more from people who need that money, because they need that.

The Bitcoin ' coin' and cryptocurrency ' currency' clearly indicate their intended use case; they're supposed to be a form of money. The first thing you think about is probably the native currency you use to buy groceries. But from where do they come? What determined these coins, bills, or numbers are worth anything on your bank account app?

The essay "Shelling Out: The History of Money," written by Nick Szabo nearly twenty years ago, is one of the more well-known documentation about the history behind money. Szabo reflects in his article on how clams, shells, beads, and precious metals in the past possessed money functions.

The technology behind cryptocurrency plays a vital role. Decentralized currencies are resistant to censorship, but even more so, just shutting them down is almost impossible.

> Node count is a reliable cryptocurrency value measure. Node count is a measure of how many active wallets there are on the network that can be searched on the Internet or a currency's homepage.

> To determine whether a currency has a fair price or not, one may check for the node count and the cryptocurrency's total market capitalization, then compare those two metrics with other cryptocurrencies.

> Supply and demand is a significant factor deciding the value of anything that can be traded, including all of the market's digital currencies. For instance, if more people try to buy bitcoins while others are willing to sell them, the price is going to go up and vice versa. And since many cryptocurrencies are restricted in availability, the increased popularity has driven up prices.

> If a currency achieves mass adoption, it can fire its value through the roof. This is because the total number of most cryptocurrencies is small, and a demand rise leads to a direct price increase.

If a fiat currency's price falls, then Bitcoin's price will increase in favor of that currency. This is because you'll be able to use your Bitcoins to get more of the money. This trend can be seen today, as more and more money has been printing by the FED, the ECB, and other central banks and artificially keeping interest rates low.

The direct costs of producing a coin and the opportunity costs are also factors that determine the worth of a cryptocurrency. For example, Bitcoin has an elevated production cost. The money and energy that were placed into bitcoin mining can be seen as a reason the bitcoin has value. It covers the manufacturing costs of specific equipment such as CPU / GPU's or servers, as well as the cooling systems for such hardware.

Although the energy used to create new Bitcoins may seem unnecessary, it's still the only way to provide users with protection-as mining is the reason why governments can't quickly shut down the Bitcoin blockchain. But there's talk among programmers about how to make the process more efficient.

Critics say transactions will be reduced and controlled due to regulations and may be seen in cryptocurrency due to a lack of security governments. Some organizations could even prohibit them as such attempts have been demonstrated in Russia and China.

How are prices calculated?

The most critical determinant of crypto-currency prices is supply and demand.

That is a fundamental economic concept. If a cryptocurrency has a high token supply and low demand from traders and consumers, then the value of the cryptocurrency may decline. Conversely, if a specific cryptocurrency's amount is small, and demand is high, then the coin's value will increase.

How do those digital currency forms compare to traditional currencies? Especially considering that there is no gold or anything else of worth behind either.

The most comfortable difference to spot between the two currencies is that centralized governments back traditional currencies. Such governments declare the legal tender for their currencies. The fiat currency value is derived from announcements by the central government. Which means everyone who owns the money puts their trust in it.

That's the case today for most countries around the world. Central banks control the money supply, foreign reserves, and the inflation rate, indirectly.

On the other hand, the cryptocurrencies do not come under a central authority or government umbrella. They are not recognized or approved as legal tender by many regions.

Also, Cryptocurrencies typically have their supply fixed, ensuring that the inflation devaluation of digital currencies is virtually non-existent.

Also, Cryptocurrencies typically have their supply fixed, ensuring that the inflation devaluation of digital currencies is virtually non-existent.

No one explicitly sets the price of Bitcoin. The market sets it, and it changes to make things even more complicated. As an example, you might look up the price of bitcoin on Google in September 2019, and might claim it was $10,099. Yet surfing for the popular bitcoin website "CoinDesk.com" on the Bitcoin Price Index could display it as $10,114. You may see a price of $10,079 on yet another platform such as "Winkdex.com"— the bitcoin price index run by the Winklevoss twins.

Part of the reason is where the data comes from for all the different values. Bitcoin is never sold in a single location. Instead, it is exchanged on multiple different markets, all of which set their average prices, depending on the transactions that the exchange makes at any given time.

Indexes collect and average prices from multiple exchanges, but not all indexes use the same transactions for their results. You can't trade bitcoin anyway through these index sites— all they do is aggregate price details.

If you are keen to buy and sell bitcoin, you have to choose a specific exchange that will have its average price. Bitcoin's price fluctuates at any given moment, depending on with whom you speak.

How fluctuate the prices of cryptocurrencies so much?

One of the main reasons why cryptocurrency prices are shifting so much is because of how new the market is. Beyond knowing the terms "blockchain" and "cryptocurrency," this area of finance is still unfamiliar to most people.

The emerging markets possess other qualities that make them competitive. Let's take a look at a few of them:

- Lack of liquidity–The crypto-currency market does not deliver as much cash compared to a traditional, established market. The gap between fiat currency and cryptocurrency in the overall market cap is over $89 trillion. That's a 36,000 percent difference.

- Daily trading rates–the regular volumes of cryptocurrency trading hover about $14 billion. On the other hand, traditional markets are at about $5 trillion.

- Thin market–Market shifts rapidly, suggesting a rise in digital currency volatility should be expected.

Early adopters–Numerous new users enter the cryptocurrency market every day. Recent reports indicate that daily more than 100,000 new adopters are part of the digital currency industry. Most new users have an interest in whether particular cryptocurrencies shift upwards or downwards. It contributes to the market's volatile nature, which leads to instability.

Price manipulation–The new BCH fork has gained prominence here. Price manipulation can be shared in new markets. Nuclear exchanges control the cryptocurrency traffic, which means they have a lot of opportunities to raise their sales. One way they do this is by manipulating cryptocurrency prices artificially. This is achieved by manipulating the market feeds shown to get traders to buy or sell particular currencies.

This kind of action and coercion is only compounded when you throw in the industry's hundreds of thousands of new participants. Such young users are easily exploited. It is difficult to prove that an unregulated market price manipulation has occurred.

How have the rates of cryptocurrencies changed in recent months?

Tracking Bitcoin's price gives us a good idea of the past 18 months' overall cryptocurrency market.

Bitcoin began at less than $1,000 in 2017 and took a dip when China revealed cryptocurrency exchange investigations in the region. At that point, most Bitcoin trading took place in China, and Bitcoin's price fell to lows of around $775, while the overall market cap for cryptocurrencies stood by approximately $15bn.

Bitcoin made a slight rebound to well over $1,000 but fell back to below $1,000 by March 2017 when the SEC refused the go-ahead for a Bitcoin ETF. The overall market cap plummeted $5 billion in two days.

Japan declared legal currency to Bitcoin in April 2017, which saw the price jump back up over $1,000. At that stage, the total market cap for cryptocurrency stood at around $26 billion.

Bitcoin steadily climbed up to $3,000 from April 2017 to July 2017, while the overall market cap went past $100 billion. Nonetheless, by mid-July 2017, the price of the Bitcoin / Bitcoin Cash split came crashing down to around $2,000 in a few short days.

The effects were short-lived, and Bitcoin recovered to nearly $5,000 by the end of August 2017, and the overall market cap on cryptocurrency came almost $170 billion.

But then, China's famously banned ICOs on Sept. 4. Nonetheless, the move induced far less correction than anticipated. Bitcoin fell to about $3,300 by mid-September 2017 but recovered quickly and hit well over $4,000 by the end of September 2017. At this point, the market cap on cryptocurrency was just under $150 billion.

The Bitcoin price gathered momentum from here. It had gone past the $6,000 mark by the end of October 2017 and finished at just under $10,000 per BTC in November 2017.

It hit highs of $20,000 in mid-December 2017, but finished the year at around $15,000, while the market cap closed the year at about $235 billion.

Bitcoin's price had come down to around $10,000 by the end of January 2018 and hit lows of $6,000 during February 2018.

We saw Bitcoin push back up past $11,000 in February 2018 and the overall market cap rising to around $500 billion — after hitting lows of about $300 billion earlier in the month.

Since then, the price of Bitcoin has been on a steady downward slope, despite occasional, short-lived recoveries, amid talks of increased regulation across the various markets, and other bumps— such as Google banning crypto advertising—. Bitcoin is trading around the $6,000 mark as of the beginning of July 2018, with the total market cap on cryptocurrencies remaining steady at around $250 billion.

Cryptocurrency Price Prediction Accuracy Just as with traditional markets, there are no guarantees, the same can be said of predictions made within the cryptocurrency market. There were those from both sides who tried to make projections for 2018 and beyond.

Some famous CEOs and pundits predicted Bitcoin would rise above the $1 million marks, while others tried to stay more modest. Still, suggesting that Bitcoin might reach $125,000 by the end of 2022 with a grain of salt should be taken.

Yet we can't always have all of the rainbows and unicorns. There are those on the other side of the market who expect nothing but doom and gloom. The economy will crash, and Bitcoin's price will drop to under $100. Some even say that before the end of the decade, it will be useless.

Regardless of the end of your continuum, there are a few things that you should keep an eye on that to help you understand better how the economy will shift. For example, if new rules and regulations are enforced on market-dominant cryptocurrencies, you may see a downward trend.

Many expected Bitcoin will hit the $1 million mark, including John McAfee (McAfee Associates), Jim Cramer of CNBC, and Bobby Lee (CEO BTCC Exchange).

Many sticks to more conservative but still important price predictions, including ex-JP Morgan chief U.S. stock strategist and current Fundstrat managing partner Tom Lee, who forecast a $25,000 price by the end of 2018 and $125,000 by 2022.

Robert Sluymer, also from Fundstrat, has set Bitcoin at just under $7,000. Bitcoin Foundation's executive director, Llew Claasen, said Bitcoin would reach $40,000.

On the other side of the scale, you partially have forecasts of a market collapse to complete. Boutique investment bank GP Bullhound forecasts a market crash of 90 percent over the year, while Harvard professor and former IMF leader Kenneth Rogoff estimated that Bitcoin would shrink to $100. Roy Sebag, CEO of GoldMoney Inc., said Bitcoin would, in the future, be worth $0.

It is quite clear that cryptocurrency price forecasts should be taken with a grain of salt. Still, there are variables to watch for that will almost certainly have an impact on Bitcoin's future price and the broader cryptocurrency market. It includes

• the scale and scope of regulations imposed on existing cryptocurrency markets

• Rate of acceptance of cryptocurrency in the coming year and beyond

• Level of development in the cryptocurrency futures market

• The utility of tokens and the potential of the underlying technology to solve real-world problems.

Note, Cryptocurrencies are still under ten years old, so the industry is in a state of affairs. There is no way to predict or decide how the market can move, but there are always indicators that can help you get a sense of what to expect.

When investing in cryptocurrencies, exercise caution, no matter what. Just because a coin that you hold today is worth hundreds or thousands, does not mean that tomorrow will be the same.

4.2 How to Invest in Cryptocurrency

These immutable and exchangeable cryptographic token promises the world as a whole to become hard and non-manipulatable money. Its supporters see a future in which Bitcoin or other cryptocurrencies will replace Euro, Dollar, etc. and create the first free and hard currency in the world.

Besides what has already been said, there are three crucial good reasons for investing in cryptocurrencies.

Second, because you want to protect your net worth against the collapse of the imperium on the dollar, which many people assume would eventually happen at some point, second, because behind cryptocurrencies, you support the social vision–that of free and hard money for the entire world. Third, because you understand the technology behind it, and like it.

There are also terrible reasons for investing in cryptocurrencies, however. Many people fall victim to the hype that surrounds each crypto-currency bubble. Always there's someone caught by FOMO (fear of missing out), buying massively in at the height of a bubble, only trying to make quick money, while not understanding cryptocurrencies. That's a wrong motive. Don't do just that. Read before spending.

Early-stage developers made millions of dollars in pure gains at Bitcoin and Ethereum. If you see the graph below, then you know exactly what we mean.

Because cryptocurrencies volatility exceeds massively that of any other investment class, they are not a typical investment. And as well as, there is always the option that your country will ban the trade and exchange of cryptocurrency. If that's the case, if you don't liquidate your crypto assets, you can make your peace. So, the important takeaway here is to lose as much money as you can afford. Like Wence Casares, Xapo's CEO sums it up in an AMA on bitcoin.com: "II still advise them [my family] that they can do the second dumbest thing right now is to own several bitcoins that they can't afford to lose and the most foolish thing they can do is not own any.

Up until late 2016 Bitcoin was the cryptocurrency, and besides that, there was not much. If you wanted to invest in cryptocurrency's success, you purchased Bitcoin. Time. Many cryptocurrencies–dubbed "Altcoins"–were penny stocks on illegal online markets, often used to keep miner's GPUs running, pump the price, and dump the coins.

There are multiple reasons for that. Although Bitcoin remains the undisputed king of cryptocurrencies, its potential usefulness has been challenged by many. First, new and exciting cryptocurrencies were coming out second, Bitcoin suffered from severe performance issues, and it looked like the Bitcoin community was nowhere near solving this issue. In particular, the block-size problem was a significant bone of contention within the group, which eventually led to bitcoin cash formation and network splitting.

The numerous websites list cryptocurrencies in diminishing market cap order. Market cap stands for the sum of all available token. It's not a perfect measure, but probably the best we've got to understand a cryptocurrency's worth.

So, have you been through the market caps and settled on the bunch of coins you'd like to invest in? Superb job. This is where, however, the real work begins.

The very first thing to do is read their whitepapers. Okay, we realize that reading PDFs might not be the most exciting thing, but you've got to put it in the effort before you get any benefits.

Reading the whitepaper itself will give you two enormous advantages:

• First, you will be more knowledgeable about the coin itself and will understand the value it brings to the environment.

• Second, a poorly written whitepaper is often a good indication of whether or not a project is worth investing in.

If the team itself cannot justify their token's real value, then investing in it is probably not worthwhile.

The bread and butter of any ICOs are a white paper.

More sincerely, a white paper will tell potential investors all they need to know about the project. This is the reason why you should simply look over an ICO that doesn't have a whitepaper.

Having said that, after reading a decently written whitepaper, you'll need to make some decisions.

Test #1: The value The Project brings in First, test the project to see if the coin brings any real utility into the ecosystem. Ethereum is a perfect example of that. There is a real excuse why it has taken so long, think about the sheer value it brought in. Developers around the world had a forum for the first time, which they could use to create their apps on a blockchain.

Also, keep in mind the problems that the crypto world desperately seeks to solve, mainly: privacy, scalability, and interoperability. An excellent way to go about your investment is to find the projects that work individually to address the issues mentioned above.

Test #2: Will need tokens for the project?

So, how do you ensure you get tokens of good quality?

You evaluate the project and ask yourself the following questions:

- Does the blockchain allow this project to be in?
- Does the project need to get tokens?

If the response for any of those happens to be "No," then those projects do not need a token, and those projects simply do an ICO to raise money. There's a way to figure out the token's real usefulness.

- Position.
- Info.
- Goal.

Cryptocurrency Exchanges are the most commonplace to buy cryptocurrency.

There are numerous exchanges to choose between, with Coinbase, GDAx, and Bitfinex among the most popular. Such transactions require you to use a debit card to buy currencies such as Bitcoin and Ethereum. You can buy fractions of a coin with the most popular currencies, including Bitcoin, so you don't have to invest billions of dollars to get into the game.

If you're interested in buying altcoins, odds are you're going to need some bitcoin or ethereum to make that buy. As a general rule, you can't purchase fiat currency altcoins (this is how crypto enthusiasts refer to paper money, like dollars or euros). Yet, in the future, that may change.

Exchanges make money by charging transaction fees, but there are other websites you can visit to connect with other users looking to sell cryptocurrencies directly. One famous example is LocalBitcoins. The process will probably be more drawn out than with exchange, and there will be an increased risk that you will deal directly with a foreigner whose currency you cannot verify. If you're new to cryptocurrencies, you're probably going to want to use an exchange.

The Bitcoin ATM is one alternative that is getting more popular. Currently, there are over 4,000 cryptocurrency ATM sites in 76 countries. You can use these to buy and transfer Bitcoin to your account.

4.3 How to start buying Bitcoins, Ethereum and other Altcoins

How do you know what type of crypto-currency to purchase? Where are you buying cryptocurrencies anyway? You are just about to find the right answers to these and other cryptocurrency investment issues.

Choose an exchange: The first thing you can do if you are involved in buying cryptocurrencies is to pick a trade. An exchange is where you can buy currencies.

Outside there are lots of different exchanges. Bitfinex and Coinbase are amongst the most famous. Currencies can be purchased with your debit card when using those exchanges.

When you buy popular currencies like Bitcoin, you can buy fractions of coins too. When you work with a limited budget, this can be a good option.

The gateway acts as one of the crypto ecosystem's most critical functions. This acts as a bridge between the Fiat world and the world of cryptography. In general, there are two types of exchanges:

- Fiat to Crypto.
- Crypto to Crypto

Fiat to Crypto exchanges: Fiat to Crypto lets you buy Cryptocurrencies in exchange for Fiat money. Coinbase is a perfect example of such exchanges. Coinbase enables you to purchase BTC, BCH, LTC, and ETH on Fiat currency exchange.

Crypto to Crypto: We then swap the Crypto to Crypto. Such exchanges help you trade those cryptos for other cryptocurrencies, such as BTC, ETH, BCH, etc. Binance is one excellent example of an exchange of crypto-to-crypto.

Although they do provide some pretty valuable resources, the problem is that they are all centralized, making them vulnerable. If you consider the sheer amount of money these exchanges deal with every single day, this is a precarious proposition.

It isn't that hard when it comes to buying Crypto from those exchanges themselves.

- First, you open an exchange account
- You then check your identity–this is necessary for most jurisdictions because of the anti-money laundering laws
- Finance your account with Dollar or Euro or whatever paper money you use. You don't need to finance your account at some exchanges, including Bitcoin.de, but trade directly with other users.

The problem, which interchange to use mostly depends on where you live. It's always better to make physically near the use of an exchange. If it is situated in the same state as you, if some bad things happen, you have the best chance to get money back legally. If there is no exchange in your jurisdiction, it is better to use exchanges with an excellent legal system based in stable countries.

You want to buy some coins, and your patience is another factor in deciding which exchange you use. If you're going to acquire large sums of Bitcoins quickly, you need to make use of one of the major exchanges that will provide sufficient liquidity. If you want to buy small amounts of coins and you're not in a rush, you should try to purchase them on short exchanges. If your order is filled out, you are likely to get better rates than on large transactions.

Allow your homework please before you decide to buy through a particular exchange and make sure it's a trustworthy exchange. There are a lot of suspicious markets that are popping up these days, and if you're not cautious, you might end up scamming.

i. Reputation Make sure you have obtained enough information about the platform, such as feedback from professional traders as well as well-known industry web sites before you launch your exchange on your selected location.

ii. Fees. Some exchanges will have information relating to taxes on their websites. Make sure you understand the exchange jargon before entering any sites: deposit, trade, and withdrawal fees. Fees can differ depending on your choice of exchange.

iii. Payment methods. Please take note of the correct way of payment. Uses the credit and debit card on the site? Switch Wire? PayPal, then? If a specific exchange has microscopic methods of payment, then this may not be convenient for you. Also note that purchasing currencies via credit card will always require Identification verification, and increases security measures come with a premium price. Please test the fees as they can be huge for using credit or debit cards.

Meanwhile, it will take longer to purchase cryptocurrency via wire transfer as it takes Banks time to process.

IV. Verification criteria for making deposits and withdrawals, most of Bitcoin's trading platforms in both the US and UK require a form of ID verification. Many exchanges also let you stay anonymous. Bear in mind that checks that take several days, but this is designed to protect exchanges from money laundering of any kind.

V. Exchange rate No wonder different exchanges offer different prices. So always try to go shopping around and not decide on an exchange immediately. It makes a big difference in your investment as, in some cases, cryptocurrency prices are known to fluctuate in value up to 10 percent and even higher.

When cryptocurrency gathers more popularity around the world, there is a vast array of sites to choose from for trading. But not all channels of trade are created equal.

Once you have found a place to buy your currencies, it's time to go shopping. There are plenty of different currencies to choose from. Still, the following are the most popular options:

- Bitcoin (BTC-USD)
- Ethereum (ETH-USD)
- Ripple (XRP-USD)
- Litecoin (LTC-USD)

Bitcoin has been caught in a bit of holding pattern lately, but it is still the most famous currency out there. Of all the people who own cryptocurrencies, Bitcoin has saved around 5 percent.

Get a crypto-currency wallet. After you've purchased your currencies, you need to position them somewhere. This place is known as your pocket. You can use two types of wallets: a software wallet and a hardware wallet.

If you want to participate in any active trading, you will need a Mobile Wallet. You will also have access to a mobile wallet when signing up for accounts with individual exchanges.

Computer wallets imitate external hard disks. You can use these to store your currency safely. These are perfect for coins you don't expect to be able to access shortly anytime.

Diversify your crypto portfolio. In the same way as diversifying your stock portfolio is safest, you should also find expanding the type of coins and currencies you are purchasing. This strategy will help shield you from the cryptocurrency world's volatile nature and protect you from significant losses.

Be vigilant of mobile wallets. You may have some people trying to convince you to use your currencies with a mobile wallet. But that is not the best approach.

Mobile devices are easy to compromise, and not as safe as they would be in a software or hardware wallet, your currencies are.

Brace for market ups and downs. Make sure to brace yourself for the cryptocurrency industry's ups and downs, too.

Don't spend more in cryptocurrencies than you're willing to lose, and brace yourself for the chance your coins ' value might fall. If you are now planning for this possibility, you will have less chance of acting out of anger or making rash decisions later.

Buying Bitcoin Without Purchasing Them: While some years ago buying cryptocurrencies was a real odyssey, today, you have a full range of options.

Let's continue with buying Bitcoin. That is the most accessible section. Many people wish to invest in Bitcoin without having to keep them.

We can use investment vehicles such as the XBT tracker (available on Swedish and German exchanges), the Second Markets Bitcoin investment trust (USA), the Bitcoin ETI (Gibraltar and Germany), and others. When Bitcoin grows, more and more brokers and exchanges are trying to set up a finance product based on Bitcoin.

All of these investment products have in common that it helps investors to bet on the price of Bitcoin without actually buying Bitcoin. While most cryptocurrency-fans believe this takes away all the fun and excitement of it, it is the easiest way for many people to invest in the future of Bitcoin. You can use the investment networks you are already used to, and you have your license and someone to take to court if something goes wrong.

At present, there is no such investment product that covers more cryptocurrencies. But some are in progress, in the US as well as in Europe.

4.4 How to make money with cryptocurrencies

There are many ways to make cryptocurrencies capital. The four most valued are:

1. You will mine them. This is where you use your computer(s) to mine for Bitcoin, i.e., to use your computer(s)'s computing power to help validate such blockchain transactions and be rewarded with Bitcoin or any other coins.

Finally, your crypto-currency coins can be mine. We're not in the days, though, where you could use your home computer to work on Bitcoin mining. Now, with so many miners working their equipment, it can be hard if you want to make money by mining using cryptocurrencies.

To get the best chance, you need to invest in graphics cards and the right setup. You need to know how to put together a machine. You'll be using more power once you get it set up. Many coins may arrive faster than others to mine. You might have more success in Litecoin mining than in Bitcoin, for example. Litecoin isn't going for as much, though. You might have something like Monero to mine too. You can get a lot of the cheaper, but then on the markets, you have to be able to sell them. If you mine something less popular, there might not be enough demand for you to sell all of your coins.

Nevertheless, no matter which tool you use to make money with cryptocurrencies, you need to be mindful of market conditions. If the value of a coin decreases, you may have to wait until it rises again to sell — or it may be a coin that doesn't turn out, and your losses are permanent. Once you start, make sure you understand the risks.

Cryptocurrency mining is one of the best ways to make money with Altcoins because it is incredibly passive: invest in the machinery, set it up, and let it run.

But there is the only problem investing in the equipment. While without extremely high-end hardware, you can mine cryptocurrency, the better the device, the quicker it can generate more coins for you, and the higher your chance of actually making money. Mining involves having computers solve mathematically complex problems, and you'll be rewarded with cryptocurrency when they solve them.

The problem is that as more blockchain is developed, the questions get more robust and harder, so if you don't have a high-end system, it can take a long time to solve things. You might also need refrigeration systems, extra power upgrades, and more to accommodate all of this.

Also, many different people try to solve the same problem simultaneously. If your machine is too sluggish, and someone else fixes the issues first, you don't get anything, and you almost always need to invest in a high-end system.

2. When you buy and hold some coins, you can lend them. This could be a great way to make money online. You can lend out your coins by using many peers to peer networks. When you do this, you will generally earn upwards of a 10 percent return on your investment.

However, as you know, there's no government or official agency controlling cryptocurrency. The lending side is the same, and you need to be extremely careful about how and to whom you lend your money.

This is where traders needing margin and leverage are borrowing your coins to sell. With a percent fee, they have to give them back to you.

3. You can purchase already established cryptocurrencies. Your first option is only to buy coins. Various exchanges allow you to buy or trade coins in your wallet to keep them in. Coinbase is amongst the most famous exchanges. Coinbase has a super clean user interface and is one of the best ways to get started if you have no previous cryptocurrencies experience. You can book free credit for $10 here!

You pay the coin market rate once you have established your account and then hold on to it until you are ready to sell. Of course, the expectation is that the price will go up.

You do need to be cautious, however, like any investment. Prices for the crypto-currency fluctuate. Bitcoin is pretty high-priced right now. You will find it hard to buy Bitcoin and have it appreciated enough. Several people are hoping to make money on cryptocurrencies by investing through Litecoin or Ethereum.

Necessarily, you'll need to make sure you're going through a trustworthy site, and back up your digital wallet. It would help if you were then cautious so that you can sell your coins when you feel that your profit has been made.

Another way to make money is to allow them for payment using cryptocurrencies. If you have a company where you are selling goods or services, you can accept payment in your preference of cryptocurrency. You need a digital wallet, and you need to deal with people who want to pay in cryptocurrency.

With a little work, you can find clients or consumers who use cryptocurrencies and are willing to pay you through the blockchain, transferring the coin to you. Nonetheless, you'll need to be able to calculate a rough estimate of what service could cost, based on the coin value. If an experienced person were to accept Bitcoin for some of their services, depending on the project, they would ask for one-fourth or one-third of a Bitcoin.

Certain currencies are, however, less valuable. If they were paid in Ethereum, they might ask for three or four ETHs. The goal is to get a feel for how your products and services translate into your chosen cryptocurrency.

You could either use it after you collect the payment to pay others for it or hang on to it until it rises in value. If the coin's value goes up, you might see a substantial profit later by selling for U.S. dollars.

4. You can buy new ICOs. New Initial Coin Offerings have recently stepped up where you can spend £ 1,000 if you get it right, and turn it into £ 10,000 or even £ 100,000 in a relatively short time. So, we will be addressing this subject as well.

Do your homework when choosing Cryptocurrencies. Don't get into the hype. When inquiring, remember to ask: 1. "Which challenge is solving it?" If it doesn't solve a problem, then why would anyone use it or buy it? And 2. "Does that problem have the right team to solve? "Bitcoin and Ethereum are the most popular, by far. Consider them as the crypto world's Reserve Currency–if you'd like to invest in other cryptocurrencies, then buy Bitcoin or Ethereum first with your local currency. Then buy the other cryptocurrencies with your Bitcoin or Ethereum. If you don't want to purchase the cryptocurrencies directly, you can always buy a Bitcoin fund or Bitcoin.

4.5 How to store and track them once you have bought them

If they say "send it to your wallet," they don't mean you put your Bitcoin in a wallet. You need a cryptocurrency wallet to store your currency, which is required to securely store the code that makes up your portfolio of cryptocurrency. You can have either a wallet with apps or a wallet with hardware. Computer wallets are needed to allow active trading, as they make it much easier to access your currency. If you register for an account with Coinbase, you will automatically receive a wallet for the Coinbase app.

Hardware wallets are physical devices–they look like USB drives a little bit–and they are better than software ones. These can be used for currencies you don't plan to need regular or secure access to. Think of a software wallet as a checking account, while your savings account is more like the hardware wallet.

The first thing you'd need to set up your digital wallet is to start investing in cryptocurrencies. In the field of cryptocurrencies, the word used is "wallet." The wallet may be likened to a bank account that can be stored on various devices.

The reason you need to do so is that there are countless stories of people who lose their cryptocurrencies. Safety is paramount here-you don't want to build a small fortune just to lose it.

A crypto-monetary wallet is a software program that works to store your private and public keys and communicate with different blockchains. It helps users to send and receive cryptocurrencies and to monitor their equilibrium.

There are a lot of wallets out there for you to choose from, which all rely on your safety needs and whether you would like to be an active trader or a more passive buy-and-hold investor (we recommend that you be a mix of the two, the so-called sweet spot).

After you have your wallet setup, you can then continue on many sites to buy and sell the digital currency of your choosing.

There are three main ways your coins can be stored:

A trade–this is the easiest way to do it, since there you are exchanging your money so that your money is kept there. Note, however, that this is an unregulated organization, and that's where most of the hacks occurred. But exchanges have been the worst place to hold your money up to now.

Keep it even better by using whatever additional security there is. For instance, Gemini not only asks for a password but also asks if you want to allow' Two-Factor Authentication' (2FA). Don't do it! It's making things even better. In case someone clones your phone, use' Google Authenticator' as opposed to text messaging, where possible.

Some of the exchanges hold your coins in cold storage for you, so theoretically, that sounds a bit safer than just keeping them on an exchange that doesn't offer that.

Cold Wallets / Storage It is called cold storage when you store your currency in a pocket that is entirely offline. Cold wallets are the way for those who want the safest type of room. These are best suited for long-term holders who for months, or years at a time, do not require access to their coins.

Not without threats of its own, but they are significantly reduced if you follow the instructions correctly and take every possible precaution. Given the amount of publicity that cryptocurrency has gained in recent years, it has, sadly, piqued attackers ' interest. In light of that, using cold storage as a means of storing your money is a far more secure option.

In hardware and paper wallets, San Francisco-based bitcoin wallet and exchange service, CoinBase holds up 97 percent of its coin reserves. What are wallets for hardware and paper? You'll find out about it in a minute.

For now, let's take a look at the pros and cons of cold storage:

Cold Storage Pros:

• A safe place to hold large amounts of coin for a long time.

• It provides a safety net against hackers and malicious-intentioned people since it is entirely offline

Cold Storage Cons are

• Still susceptible to external damage, theft, and general human carelessness.

• Not ideal for quick and regular transactions.

• Setting newcomers up can be a little daunting.

2. A Hot Wallet. This is harder to hack, and therefore more secure than an exchange. Nonetheless, it can still be compromised, as it is online. It also means more work because, for each of the different coins, you have to open up several wallets. It's a pain, but it does. Better be safe than sorry.

There will be two ways of doing that:

1. The ones that store your online public key and private key, and

2. These set up online but hold your private keys on your PC or mobile phone.

In simple terms, Hot Wallet / Storage Hot storage is when you store your cryptocurrency in a wallet with a direct internet connection. This link is what makes a "soft" computer

As a hot wallet, you should think of exchanging wallets, desktop customers, and mobile wallets (any wallet that resides on a smartphone that will ever connect to the Internet). Accessing funds on a hot wallet is simple, and if you live somewhere that supports micropayment cryptos, there's nothing wrong with using one for day-to-day expenses. Think of it as fiat (currency issued by the government). You could walk around in a wallet for convenience with a portion of your money, but most of you are safely away. Similar to a real-world wallet, your hot wallet will act. For ease of access, you use it to hold a small amount of cash. That is everything.

While it's straightforward to transact with hot wallets, there's a massive drawback to them. They are easy to hack. Recently, the entire crypto-space has gained much value and, where there is value, crime is never far behind. Recent ransomware attacks and earlier significant exchange vulnerabilities should be enough beacons for newcomers.

Even if you're not going to store a lot of value on your hot wallet, you must follow the backup steps within your wallet's restore section to avoid losing funds by human error. With your private key, and the seed phrase intact, you should be able to restore any pocket painlessly.

Hot Storage Pros

- Easy access to funds.

- Wide range of products and support for various devices.

- User-friendly UIs allow secure sending and receiving.

Hot storage Cons

- Exposed to cybercrime. A constant threat is advanced hackers, ransomware, and other malicious actors.

- The computer could be damaged, and the wallet lost. You could permanently lose your investment in cryptocurrency without carefully backing up private keys and seed terms.

- Documentation of the reconstruction could still be lost/damaged/stolen.

Now let's explore the various kinds of wallets you can use for hot storage.

- Wallets aka Cloud Wallet
- Mobile Wallets
- Desktop Wallets
- Wallets Multisig

1. Online or Cloud Wallet There's no turning back once you've used www.myetherwallet.com. It is effortless to use, of course, once you've used it a few times: —)

2a. Desktop PC / Mac Wallet This is accessible by hackers depending on how secure your desktop is or isn't, i.e., if your PC gets a virus, then people can hack it to get your private keys.

2b. Mobile wallet Jaxx is the most popular mobile wallet. This synchronizes with your laptop and phone so that you can back up your private key. This can be downloaded from the App Store or Google Play. Www.jaxx.io Jaxx is excellent as it stores many different coins all in one, such as Bitcoin, Ethereum, Litecoin, Dash, etc.

3. An offline Wallet, a.k.a. Cold storage or hard storage–this is where your private key is stored on a special USB stick, so it's off-grid. Once offline, hacking is practically impossible. If the cleaner throws it out, however, then you lose it for good. And yes, this has happened with people losing $millions of hard disks thrown out by mistake.

The most famous are: Trezor: this was the first hard wallet in its original form.

They're SIMPLE to use as most of these systems but not easy to use. It's like climbing a mountain for the first time, but after that, every use becomes more comfortable and more relaxed.

You'll be an absolute expert there soon, showing off to all your colleagues. If you did not die first time climbing the mountain, that is — Ledger Nano S: one of the most popular ones.

The Ledger is seemingly popular with people. It's almost the same as the Trezor, but it looks better and cheaper. I guess those are two good reasons to buy something, mainly since it's pretty much the same as the Trezor.

KeepKey: Keepkey has a bigger screen, but I haven't used it myself. With all of the above, you have to find out the number that you think it's safer to put on there, i.e., some coins worth more than $25,000 in value I use a cold storage wallet.

4. Wallet Paper. This is where you write down a piece of paper, literally, your private key. That is much cheaper than buying one of the above, of course.

Make sure you keep a copy because your private key is lost once the document is destroyed and your coins are gone.

Implement these three Laws, with all of the above:

1. Please back up your wallet, no matter what one you're using.

2. If using the app, keep the program up to date.

3. Use whatever extra security, such as two-factor Authentication, is available. In case someone copies your account, using Google Authenticator as opposed to text messaging, where possible.

Without question, using a paper wallet is the easiest way to store any crypto-currency. You could set one up absolutely free of charge by following a few references below. That makes you the master of your property, and if precautions are taken, there is no chance that anyone else will know your private keys. This, of course, means it's even more important to keep a record of them.

Losing private keys means you're going to lose your paper wallet's entire content (but then again, that's valid for every wallet out there). To keep it very plain, paper wallets are an offline cold storage option to save crypto-currency. This involves printing out your private and public keys in a piece of paper that you will then store and keep in a secure place. The keys are printed as QR codes, which you will be able to scan for all your transactions in the future. It is therefore so safe that it gives you, the user, complete control. You don't need to worry about a piece of hardware's well-being, nor do you need to worry about hackers or any aspect of malware. You need to have a piece of paper looked after.

How do you monitor them once you buy them?

"If you can't measure it, you can't make it better."- Management thinker Peter Drucker There are several sites you can use to track your cryptocurrencies once you've purchased them.

Online numerous websites and applications are available to help you manage your crypto for free.

You can either put in what you purchased manually, or you can cut and paste code from the exchange in, and it will automatically do it. This way, it has common variations of all the coins. This is a perfect way to track all of your stocks, even if they're at multiple exchanges or wallets. You don't want to log in every day to various exchanges.

4.6 When to buy and sell

"THE ONLY PEOPLE WHO LOSE MONEY ARE THE ONES THAT HAVE TO SELL." - WARREN BUFFETT

It is not a general rule when buying cryptocurrencies. Usually, buying in at the height of a bubble isn't a good idea, and generally, buying it when its crashes isn't a good idea either. Never catch a falling knife, as the wisdom of the trader notes. The best time could be for the price to be stable at relatively low levels.

It is deciding when a crypto is in bubble mode, and when it reached the bottom after dropping is the art of trading. In the present, what is easy to say in retrospect is a tough question which can never be answered with absolute certainty. Sometimes a coin begins to rise, and after a mark passes, where everyone thinks this must be a bubble's peak, the real rally just starts.

For instance, a lot of people didn't buy Bitcoin at $1,000 or Ether at $100, because it seemed crazily expensive. But a few months later those rates seem to have been a good starting point.

There are only two pieces of advice we can give regarding timing. Next, don't equate crypto bubbles with conventional bubbles in finance. It's not a bubble 10 percent up, but it can be uncertainty every day. One hundred percent up can be a bubble, but it's often just the beginning. Typically, 1,000 percent could be a bubble, but there's no guarantee it will pop.

Secondly, take some watching time. Don't buy-in, for there was a dip. There could be another one. And don't buy-in, for you're afraid it'll blow tomorrow. Watch it, get informed, buy it, if you think the timing is right. Then, most importantly, perhaps: don't be a weak hand. Don't sell out too fast. Keep on. The monetary upheaval has just started.

When you buy cryptocurrency to invest it, gift it, or donate it, then you're going to want to buy it before you intend on using it. When is the best time, exactly? Like many financial decisions, it depends on a lot of factors: which cryptocurrency you're buying, the reason you're buying it, your financial condition, and the overall cryptocurrency market's current state— just to name a few.

Don't invest when it comes to investing in altcoins while the coin is on the rise!

How to Invest in Cryptocurrency: When not buying

1. Of course, the Price is High, that's why you have to learn about it. People don't get to know about cryptography until they start performing correctly?

Similarly, until they start making some waves, you can't hear about those cryptos, but then, I'm telling you this isn't just an excellent time to buy, and it's just because the price is high. Why spend big when you can purchase low??

That now brings us to the second level.

2. Chill. The price is still going to come down, and this is real, indeed. That is what they are all doing. They're just going to rise and fall even in-between minutes, so what's the rush when you know that? You find it makes sense to wait for those coins to fall a little or at least settle down before you go for them.

3. You don't want to go swimming to join the Destination Cruise!

Now that means, you don't want to buy A HIGH PRICE when it's rising and then... All of a sudden, it's just starting to crash again [as described in point 2 above] It's about the worst thing that can happen to you... selling off your Bitcoins to get an altcoin and the next day it's dropping.

Or at least, you'll be emotionally and physically exhausted because you are going to want to sell it again and buy Bitcoins! Trust me that you don't want to do it.

So how does one successfully invest?

THERE'S NO ANSWER TO IT.

HOWEVER, don't generally buy why:

1 when it's not Through the crypto or

2. When that falls, or 3. It's the best time to buy these things when it's safe and this way you won't be surprised by unexpected changes in what could come next.

Don't buy cryptocurrencies when they're RACING up the hill because they're going down the valley forever.

This is the holy grail of trade -WHEN to get out of business.

We are as a technology at the start of cryptocurrencies, so there could be huge upside potential. We are looking upwards to the limit. If there's one thing, I've discovered it's that if you want to make a lot of money, you have to let your winners fly. We're holding the upside potential for the long term.

A few things to know when it's time to go — signs selling your Bitcoin is time.

You made it to your target!

Following one of the basic principles of trading, you need to sell it for more than you bought it for to make a profitable investment. It's your time to sell when the price of Bitcoin rose to its highest after you decided to buy Bitcoin— it's called your time-high. The best choice is to set a target — if the demand hits a specific high time, you're considering selling. You can also set up stop-loss alerts in most of the digital currency exchanges, so you always know when your investment has hit your target.

You don't even know what Bitcoin is.

Your mate, boy, colleague, and neighbour told you Bitcoin is the better investment than any word, but you still don't know what it is? Each time you try to grasp blockchain, do you get a headache? If the crypto market, even for a short-term investment, seems too difficult to manage, then it may be time to sell. When you can't see the time coming big, then there's no point in holding on.

You get worried about your money.

There are many reasons why people think about Bitcoin. Sometimes, Cryptocurrency charts look like the artistic kid who took his crayons to a wall in your house. Prices rise, leap, and shifts are nearly unpredictable. Such ups and downs can be a cause of some severe anxiety, as when you wake up in the morning, you never know how much your assets are going to be worth. You'll continue to contemplate whether you've traded peaks at the right time or if you've been waiting longer for a day if you've been able to get a better Bitcoin price. Then you are in a panic, and you sell everything out of rage. Cryptocurrency trading is not for the heartless, and if these situations sound familiar, it is perhaps a sign that it is time to sell your Bitcoin. There's no future bitcoin, term investment, or digital currency worth that much fear.

Another way, the grass is greener.

Is there a project that appealed to you and that you want to get into? Is it an investment in a brand-new term? Sail back! For financing, we have to put our money where we think there is an excellent opportunity (in the realm of reason, of course). A lot of companies are looking for investors and ICOs that pledge ground-breaking projects so that you can find your Bitcoin some other place. Who knows what? It could be a better investment for the term than potential bitcoin! The only important thing is to ensure that you do your due diligence, scope out your investment opportunity, know everything about the founders, the industry, the product, etc. Sometimes, behind fake projects, there are malicious actors just waiting for you to send them your digital currency option so they can con you out. Don't let them do that!

Your whole wealth is in Bitcoin.

There's a fact you can't deny: Cryptocurrencies are a risky investment. Whether it's going to turn out to be the biggest bubble of all time or a huge investment, we can't know at this point, and the market still shows enormous swings in the overall crypto price. All of your one-day savings in Bitcoin could mean $100 and $50 the next day. You don't know when the Bitcoin price hits the time-high. This is incredibly risky, and even in the short term, it is a wrong investment decision. Diversify your investments, take it as a sign that it's time to sell your Bitcoin, and get out of it. Just hold in crypto as much as you can afford to lose, because if you don't ask, "Does Bitcoin fail?" you could wind up broke.

There can be tricky things in everybody's life for our wallets. Bitcoin could be a considerable investment or merely a bubble. There are certainly more important life events than the ones on Bitcoin exchanges. If you need some cash in your life for a critical case and not a Cuban holiday, then sell your Bitcoin, particularly if you still have a long-term profit.

You've got all the gold and no care.

And don't you even know the price of Bitcoin anymore? Caution is key to handling cryptocurrencies. The crypto market's high volatility, with technological changes, hacks, inventions, and legislation around every corner, means the market is ever-evolving. Every day you don't want to wake up just to know your Bitcoin assets have fallen to below sea level. The only way to keep a wise decision on your long-term investment is to keep up with the market always. If you don't want to spend a bit of your time, long-term, and every day exploring crypto, it might be better not to do it at all. Take it as a sign that it's time to sell your crypto, and find some other long-term or short-term investment that will help you keep track of.

You expect divine intervention to tell you it is time to sell your Bitcoin.

There's no global time to sell Bitcoin, so nobody can tell you exactly when to sell. This is how the market works— if everyone starts selling, the price will fall, and your investment will sink in the next moment. You need to rely on your expertise, trading experience, market knowledge, and some luck in digital currency trading to know that your investment has reached the highest possible price. So, if the price has hit a time-high, you've been studying the market and rationally judging it as the best price reasonable, it's a sign to sell your Bitcoin!

You'll need to consider things like your investments, your risk tolerance, the tax consequences, and why you purchased crypto when deciding on when to sell (or not). When you work out the answers, what you will find is that your situation— like the situation of everybody — is unique, meaning that there is no universal "right" time to sell cryptocurrency.

Crypto markets never close, as opposed to the stock market. You can sell cryptocurrency at any time. It's up to you entirely.

Although Blockchain's whole idea is independence, security, and decentralization, it doesn't mean that all the risks are demolished. Sure, your Bitcoins and Altcoins funds are better protected than they are in traditional banking systems. But many fraudulent schemes have already reached the underlying network.

So, tip

#1: use multiple exchanges. Lower fees, user-friendly interface, the range of methods of payment, advanced account security are key factors you should consider.

#2 Do not rush to swap fiat currency coins and then withdraw to your bank account. More stores and businesses gradually embrace Bitcoins and some other altcoins.

#3 Trust the rhythm of the company as a beginner. Choose the most popular markets, sites for trading, and coins. What's suitable for most, won't hurt your interests.

Eventually, with some experience gained, depending on your selling/buying intentions, you will be competent enough to make the necessary decisions.

And finally, #4-never forget to make your private/public essential backup.

4.7 Asset allocation and how much to invest in cryptocurrencies

How much should digital currency become a portfolio for an investor?

This depends on a great many factors, including risk tolerance and experience with cryptocurrencies.

In these digital assets, an investor might put a small fraction of his portfolio within.

Instead, he might spend a much more significant amount, setting himself up for the enormous potential for upside but also more chance of downside.

Before a person even thinks about investing in cryptocurrencies, they should be following some basic principles.

For example, "never bring more into crypto than you can afford to lose," said Jacob Eliosoff, a manager of the crypto-monetary fund.

"This is all still very dangerous," he underlined.

"If you can't laugh wryly and move on if it goes to $0, you should never have gotten in." Eliosoff's argument is essential, as some investors poured significant amounts of their savings into digital currencies during the market boom, only to see the value of those assets fall when the bubble bursts, "You're a fool if you don't invest in crypto assets," said Tim Enneking, managing director of Digital C.

At the same time, he stressed caution, suggesting that "if you spend too much, you're also a fool." Several other experts recommended that investors only make small allocations to digital currencies, placing no more than 10 percent of their portfolio into these destructive properties.

"A 3-5 percent allocation of cryptography is appropriate" in the age mentioned above range for a "young professional," said David Martin, chief investment officer at U.S. asset manager Blockforce Capital.

Virtual assets are "uncorrelated to any other asset class," he added, "so they do well to improve diversification in our highly correlated and ever-increasing global markets." Similar figures were listed by Joe DiPasquale, CEO of cryptocurrency hedge fund BitBull Capital.

"I'd say between 0 per cent-5 percent of the portfolio being in crypto is a good start" for a long-term saving young person.

He added that "if possible," the portfolio "should be managed on an annual basis depending on how the market matures." Marouane Garcon, managing director of Amulet's crypto-to-crypto derivatives company, also weighed in, saying: "Because of the volatility and uncertainty of crypto, I would still make it a small part of my overall portfolio," adding that "anywhere around 5-10%" of one's entire section.

Some market observers suggested making allocations to digital assets more sizeable.

Greenspan presented statistics slightly more aggressively than some of the other analysts who contributed to this article.

"An investor may bring" between 6 and 18 percent "into cryptocurrencies, depending on the size and composition of the portfolio as well as the risk tolerance.

Scott Weatherill, Chief Risk Manager of B2C2 Japan, said that "I think 20 percent is very fair, but I would also add that it is better just to buy BTC and ONLY BTC." "It dramatically simplifies all tax headaches in and out of altcoins (given the current legal landscape) and is likely to outperform the more extensive space given favourable dynamics of scarcity (low inflation compared to b)

Eliosoff said that "people who follow closely enough" to know the difference between Bitcoin and Bitcoin cash, for instance, could bring "up to 33 percent of their portfolio into cryptocurrencies. Marius Rupsys, a digital currency trader, also gave some scenarios under which investors could make significant allocations to crypto-assets.

4.8 What is ICO (Initial Coin offering)

An ICO (Initial Coin Offering) is a method of fundraising that trades future cryptocurrencies coins that have immediate, liquid value. Just as an IPO is an initial public offering when a private firm wants to go public on an exchange, an ICO is an initial coin offering. Initial Coin Offerings or ICOs are necessarily crowded sales, the crowdfunding version of the cryptocurrency.

The only difference is that the start-up sells tokens on a blockchain in an ICO while IPO sells shares. It usually occurs before the launch of a blockchain coin and involves the public sale, or crowd sale, of a percentage of the initial supply of the coin. ICOs are sometimes referred to as ICPOs or ITOs (Initial Token Offerings) or even a' Crypto Crowdsale.' The start-ups are called' Blockchain Start-ups ' themselves.

Many of the firms that run ICOs don't sell coins but tokens instead. And tokens and coins are all very different stuff. Coins, like Bitcoin, are a form of monetary value transfer. On the other side, tokens can store complex and multifaceted streams of data that can be used for endless functionality.

Many of the new companies that hold ICOs are not currencies and will be built on the blockchain instead of technology. So, they cannot be judged solely on their monetary value, but rather based on their business model and the potential solution they need to be measured.

Where within an ICO is the so-called' white paper'? Every ICO should have a manifesto or white paper. For example, at the back of this book lies the original Bitcoin white paper (see appendices). It details how the system is intended to work, how the tokens are constructed, and how the tokens could be received and used by the users. A white paper shows if the creators have been working through the idea, what problem it solves, and how it means to solve it. Crucially, it also needs to show how the tokens they give out will be used to solve the problem, as you'll own some in return for investment.

What performs an ICO?

1. A company adverts it will be selling its new cryptocurrency's initial coin supply.

2. Investors are reading the start-up's' white paper' and exchanging Bitcoin or Ether for those new coins on that basis.

The start-up can then swap your Bitcoin or Ether into standard fiat currency to spend on building up the technology, paying for costs, etc. 4. If the project is a success, that is to say, it launches and begins to be adopted, then the value of the new currency rises, and ICO investors make a profit.

Why do they do businesses? ICO provides them with a more straightforward and quicker means of funding than a traditional method for new blockchain ventures. It's also border-free to be able to connect with every investor in the world.

A percentage of the tokens are usually sold to ICO participants, and a portion is retained for the needs of the business (private investors, etc. Definitions vary from one ICO to the next).

How to make money at an ICO? Many investors hope the company will be profitable enough to launch an exchange, so they can sell their tokens or coins to benefit as soon as possible. We don't necessarily believe in the business itself, or they may find in the product, but they aren't willing to risk long-term remaining in if they can make 100-1000 percent in the short term.

Are there risks to investing in ICOs? Yes, there are lots of them.

The start-up idea is written on a' white paper'–often without any work proof–and people are investing based on what they read in the white paper. Because investors pour in their money, hoping to become rich through ICOs, some of these ICO start-ups take advantage of this situation. They collect the money but don't really get to the job of creating the commodity, thus transforming the company into a profit-making operation on its own. Then they disappear into the ether.

Mycelium ICO was an exceptionally ill example of this. After raising the money, its team members just vanished, and later it was reported that they used the funds to pay for their vacation.

There is so much talk of controlling and automatic. That is why.

Those who are genuine and want to create a product may have the question of inadequate technological or support knowledge. We may be underqualified and lack the Blockchain business building experience.

4.9 Is Cryptocurrency Taxable

Nothing is certain except death and taxes. The same with cryptocurrencies persists. If you are making money by investing in cryptocurrencies, you will probably have to pay the vat. Everything else is as it is.

Whether you need to tax the returns on investments in cryptocurrencies is up to your national tax authority.

The Good News. The issue of cryptocurrency and taxation is good news. Next, cryptocurrencies are VAT excluded in almost every country in the world. You don't need to pay VAT on Bitcoin sale, just like with any financial product. There have been some proposals of tax authorities in Poland, Estonia, Germany, Australia, and Sweden seeking VAT on crypto transactions. Still, after this was smashed down by the European Court in a significant decision, VAT for Bitcoins seems to have become a non-theme.

The good news is that you have to pay close to no taxes in some jurisdictions. Incredibly Germany became a tax haven for cryptocurrencies, a country which is usually known for very high tax rates. Like the USA and many other countries, Germany finds Bitcoin a property rather than a financial product. It means that if you earn money by trading it, you don't pay a flat tax on business income–which is 25 percent on bank account interest, for example–but you have to charge the benefit of buying and selling like income cryptocurrencies.

It's more like you were selling your house than a safe.

You purchased 10 Bitcoins for EUR 1000 and traded them for EUR 2,000? Your taxable income was up 10,000 Euros.

When the price was 1,000 Euro, you bought one bitcoin for 100 Euro and ordered a 10-Euro-Pizza? Your income was up 9 Euros. The tax rate for that is higher in most situations than for financial gains.

There's one exception, though. When you keep your coins for more than one year when you sell them, you don't have to pay any taxes at all. The provision was introduced to prevent the day-to-day exchange of other assets and to maintain rates by facilitating holders. It made Germany, and also the Netherlands, which applied the same rules to tax havens for cryptocurrencies. Some countries may have regulations similar to these. Your tax consultant can help you out, in doubt.

One question that the one-year rule raises is that you need to show you're keeping the crypto for this time frame. Exchanges typically can assist with your trade history prints. Also, the public blockchain can be used as proof of storage. In most cryptocurrencies, it is clear when a single address receives coins and spends them. Yet, not in anything.

Monero, for example, uses Ring Signatures and Confidential Transactions, which are perfect tools to keep anonymity. But the downside is that they find it more or less impossible to prove you have more than a year of carrying coins. You might consider this when selecting coins for your portfolio.

Chapter 5: Strategies

"After spending a lot of years in Wall Street, and having made and lost billions of dollars, I want to inform you this: it was never my thought that made me big money. It was my sitting all the time. Was it? My sitting uptight! "Jesse Livermore, Millionaire Trader.

Once your accounts have been opened, you will start investing in the coins.

Just a plan is all you need now. Many people don't have an idea they've thought about beforehand, written down, and then implemented in the message.

By 2020, anyone can make huge profits by investing by cryptocurrencies. Only spend at the right time— as in December 2017, when nobody could fail.

But it takes luck to invest at the right time. Only those who daily develop their investment strategy for cryptocurrencies, error after mistake, always smash the masses.

As a new investor in cryptocurrencies, kicking off your shoes and taking your first steps along The Blockchain's Route, you've probably found yourself asking the following questions: did the bitcoin bubble burst, is it too late to get started, and what are the best tips for success in this newly emerging investment space?

5.1 What are the typical investment strategies

Creating a Cryptocurrency investment strategy can be difficult as a reasonably young investment group.

These are five steps anyone can take to build the ultimate investment strategy for the cryptocurrency.

#1 Knowing the market Cryptocurrencies may imitate traditional financial assets. Still, they are undeniably exceptional, acting both as a forward-looking representation of natural products and, at the same time, as an ultimate innovation.

The cryptocurrencies are infamously unpredictable, for example.

Erratic and sometimes unexplainable spikes in prices are typical for the crypto investor course. This practice has provided add-ons to the lexicon. "HODL," a misrepresentation that has become a mantra for crypto investors, is intended to ease the fears of investors as uncertainty inevitably comes in.

What's more, cryptocurrencies are a global phenomenon, suggesting that at the same time, they are subject to the laws and standards and the various nations. It's a part of the crypto revolution that is becoming more apparent over time, but it's one that investors need to recognize before they trust the sector to their financial future.

The crypto world is, of course, full of quirks that will set the parameters for a successful investment strategy.

#2 Develop a diversified portfolio. Bitcoin is the most popular cryptocurrency with nearly 90 percent name recognition but not the only asset available.

Thousands have been made available in digital currencies after cryptocurrencies became a global phenomenon in 2017. Each project has its intent and functionality, and together they represent an opportunity to create a diversified portfolio of investments.

A diversified portfolio, widely known as the most critical component of any investment strategy, acts as a buffer against uncertainty while taking advantage of the growth markets.

Achieving diversity in crypto markets can, in some respects, be more complicated than traditional sources of investment. For one, though hundreds of cryptocurrencies are available to choose from, these assets are distributed over dozens of different cryptocurrencies. Although third-party platforms may help investors integrate these assets into a single screen, the method may not be as intuitive as it is elsewhere.

Although betting on the proliferation of single crypto can be enticing, wise investors must diversify their strategy to minimize risk and seize the opportunity.

#3 Use your capital. Traditional investment strategies have dramatically changed in the digital age, regardless of industry. It's getting more automated.

More than 90 percent of their investment services are focused on automated trading processes at investment juggernaut Goldman Sachs, making the in-person machination a thing of the past.

At the same time, issues like social trading are becoming more popular, a practice that allows inexperienced investors to execute the actions of more expedited traders instantly.

This is excellent news for investors looking to build their investment strategy for cryptocurrencies because many of these same resources are also used in crypto markets.

For example, CryptoHopper allows crypto investors with different experience levels to use their automated trading bot to conduct algorithmic trading strategies. Investors can also subscribe to copy the trading methods that enable unfamiliar investors to pursue the same approach as more mature participants in the market.

It is easy for anyone to start developing a robust investment portfolio that includes the emerging asset class of cryptography by using the available resources.

#4 Choose the best platforms. To produce a fantastic crypto portfolio, you need to choose the exchanges and wallet services that suit your needs.

Fortunately, there's no shortage of options for consumers.

Today, there are more than 500 exchanges in cryptocurrency that each imbue their personal touch with the crypto-ecosystem. Likewise, several wallet services can help any investor store their portfolio and handle it.

Every product is full of its own set of complexities, but investors can, in general, value certain aspects more than others. Expressly, priority must be provided to interoperability, and security usability features. If you are struggling to choose a platform, consider some of the tools and feedback that can help you select the platform that is right for you.

#5 Be consistent. Finally, the linchpin of the plan will not be one single component of the crypto investment strategy. Alternatively, consistency is expected when constructing a portfolio of crypto investments, such as building a traditional investment portfolio.

So, make regular contributions to your assets that have been allocated. Cryptocurrencies can be nowadays the hottest investment class. Nevertheless, they aren't a get-rich-quick scheme, and buying digital tokens like lottery tickets might help some people make sumptuous headlines. Also, it won't let most investors develop a long-term investment strategy for cryptocurrencies.

That's why Fidelity Investments, one of the world's most prominent investment banks, urges their customers to make ongoing contributions to their investments, adding, "When you invest consistently over months, years, and decades, short-term downturns won't have a big impact on your overall results."

Creating the ultimate portfolio on cryptocurrencies will not occur overnight. Nonetheless, when investors understand the market's intricacies, diversify their assets, use their capital, and use the best channels, they can continually grow this asset, which could produce the vigilant investor's incredible return.

5.2 Which investment strategy is right for me

Here are a few general approaches for investing that may suit you.

Go all - in and HODL (try to avoid this one): the simplest thing to do today goes all - in and then "just HODL." The problem with this strategy is that it's like walking up to the roulette table and putting everything on black. That's true, but there's no complexity in the plan. If you do not manage to time the absolute bottom of the market, you will end up watching your on-paper capital disappear without many choices to do more than cut losses or wait.

Establishing an overall average, and then HODL: This is a conservative and straightforward technique that helps remove worries about the regular prices. Either you buy irrespective of the price at regular intervals, or you buy incrementally as if the price is down over time. This helps to avoid mistiming the market by creating an extended duration over months or even years. You can take some or all of them in between as you see gains here and there (and then reinvest those later if and when you see more attractive prices). Often, one would possibly want to leave roles slowly. Over time, slowly entering and leaving positions helps you to mitigate risk when investing.

This can be a robust High-Risk Strategy, unpredictable reward asset such as Bitcoin. You could end up paying long-term capital gains tax as a bonus rather than the short-term tax (it's about 1/2 as much), and you're going to avoid some of the headaches of disclosing complicated crypto-tax traders.

Trade, targets at buying low and selling high: To do this, you needn't know more than just how to buy and sell crypto. Purchase at rates you think are small, like whatever the price after a few days of falling prices, then try to sell when prices are higher. You can either set stop losses if you get it wrong, or you can "hold bags" (mainly reverting to a policy of "build an average position and hold" if you get it wrong). If you like to do it like a pro, then study Technical Analysis (TA) is required. TA allows you to base your buy and sell on support levels, moving averages, etc. If you get it right, TA will help you boost the profitability of your trades, but if you get it wrong, it could psych you out. Watch out for commissions and portfolio depletion if you do an exchange.

Use a Trading bot to deal: Trading bots are apps designed to handle your trades. The real benefit is that while you are sleeping, it can do your bidding. Sleeping puts all the tension out. If you're going to trade, the time and effort and resources needed to get a bot up and running is likely worth it. You don't have to do something fancy with it, just let it put stop losses for you, or if you know any simple TA, try making it trade stuff like death crosses and golden crosses on 2hr+ candles (this technique is popular enough that you need to watch out for any time frame, if everybody automates this without any additional parameters, then each crossover will be more unforgettable than it already is).

Do A Mix of the Above: A mix of the above can be made to play it safe when learning about and enjoying everything that cryptocurrency has to offer. In investment mode, you can have one instance of your bot, one in trade mode, you can trade a little by hand, and you can store the rest of your funds in a safe offline wallet. Perhaps your wallet exceeds all your other good intentions, and maybe your bots will save you from your emotional trade? Here's the thing, if one thing works very well for you and the others aren't, now you know what kind of investor/trader you might want to concentrate on being.

Chapter 6: Opinion about Cryptocurrency

Bitcoin and other virtual currencies, AKA cryptocurrencies or only cryptocurrency, are creating significant confusion in the financial domain. Its value is determined by a blockchain or complex code that can be exchanged between multiple computers but is anonymous and independent of any issuer from the government. This makes crypto appealing for both valid (e.g., supply chain transactions between a company and its suppliers) and illegal (drug money laundering) usage.

Bitcoin has experienced the tremendous highs and lows of any invention over the past decade, whether in terms of security problems, rivals, and significantly fluctuating demand rates.

All of which led to blockchain and bitcoin, and an extent to alternative forms of cryptocurrencies, hitting common knowledge.

While some economic experts believe that cryptocurrency has excellent potential, others feel that it is a highly inflated asset similar to other past bubbles, will these alternative currencies eventually replace conventional currencies and become as omnipresent as dollars and euros one day? Or are cryptocurrencies a fad that's going to flame out soon?

The solution to that is Bitcoin.

6.1 What the Pros Think About Crypto

Let's look at some of the forecasts made by market traders or experts:

- Venture capital investor-Tim Draper has predicted that the total market capitalization for cryptocurrencies will reach $80 trillion over the next 15 years.

- At a press conference in Buenos Aires, JP Morgan CIO Lori Beer said that blockchain would "replace existing technology" in the coming years, adding that JP Morgan uses blockchain technology to simplify the payment process and store customer information relevant to KYC (Know Your Consumer) policy.

- Kim Dotcom, an entrepreneur, and MegaUpload founder reiterated his confidence in Bitcoin over fiat currency, telling fans to "buy bitcoin" directly, and warning them not to purchase dollar as it will become useless.

- Robert Kiyosaki-the author of "Rich Dad, Poor Dad," the best-selling financial novel, expressed his concern that cryptocurrencies would eventually replace US dollars. (Cryptocurrency Future of Money)

- The CEO of the world's largest stock exchange-NYSE says that bitcoin has the potential to be the world's "first world currency," and throws the weight of his business behind an ambitious plan to make that a reality.

Now, let's look at the use cases and how the institutions are accepting cryptocurrencies: Cryptocurrency Future Worldwide.

- IBM, Citi, CLS, Barclays formed a partnership to create blockchain app stores for banks. LedgerConnect-a Distributed Ledger Technology (DLT) platform is the result of a collaboration between foreign exchange settlement provider CLS, corporate software giant IBM, and nine financial institutions, including big names including Citigroup and Barclays.

- Blockchain company based in Singapore-CyClean is introducing a blockchain-enabled fleet of electric vehicles that would allow crypt as users drive. The business seeks to reduce carbon emissions and compensate individuals for doing so.

• Samsung SDS, Samsung Group's IT portion, recently announced that it would be actively using its Nexledger blockchain platform to develop Korea Customs Service's export clearance program.

• Iran has announced that cryptocurrency mining will start to be handled as an industry; The legislation comes after increased pressure on the government, prompted by a shift in U.S.-imposed economic sanctions.

• Tech giants Alibaba and IBM are battling for the top spot on a new list that ranks global companies by the number of patents on blockchain filed to date. China's Alibaba seals first place, having filed a total of 90 patent applications related to blockchain, while IBM has recorded a total of 89 to date. Mastercard is in third place— with 80 filings led by Bank of America with 53.

• The new Builderium project, based in Switzerland, is creating a global platform to make deals and compare parties to carry the advantages of the digital economy to the growing market for building. The company expects the US construction market shortly to hit $773 billion as the product is global, so the consumer is not limited to either regional or national markets.

• The Australian government has allocated A$ 2.25 million ($1.7 million) to the Sustainable Sugar Project, led by the Queensland Cane Growers Association, used to track the provenance of sugar supplies to Australia-the Smart Cane Best Management Practice (SMP) program.

• The Medical School in New York, founded by Mount Sinai Hospital, has launched a new research centre focused on blockchain healthcare technologies that explore the application of artificial intelligence, robotics, genomic sequencing, sensors and wearable devices in medicine. (The future of crypto-currency in the United States).

• Major Cineplex, Thailand's largest cinema chain, is reportedly introducing crypto payments that allow customers to pay for crypto products and services, including tickets and popcorn. The Thai Securities and Exchange Commission even began accepting the crypto operators ' license applications.

• Kaliningrad, one of the cities which hosted the FIFA World Cup, is now offering cryptocurrency payments for hotel rooms. (Cryptocurrency future in Russia).

These use cases and forecasts talk much about and even after the future of cryptocurrencies in 2020. Space for the blockchain (the technology behind cryptocurrencies) is growing faster than ever before. As these organizations and technologies mature, their cases of real-world use will multiply, more than we see today, reducing some speculative market elements to ground it in the actual performance, utility, form, and function of the next generation of the Internet. We succeeded in adding to some of the implementation instances, but there are many more.

6.2 Are there any drawbacks to investing in cryptocurrencies

Cryptocurrencies have several drawbacks, particularly with ICOs. This is an entirely new and unregulated business, meaning you won't get paid if you're hacked, and someone steals your Bitcoins. Also, new coin releases are that, and no one knows which ones will vanish and which ones are here to stay. Because of this volatility, price fluctuations of 30 per cent+ are not unusual in a single day up or down. So, at the moment, you're just investing money that you're willing to lose.

Overall, there are four Cryptocurrencies disadvantages. This digital currency is lacking incomprehension. Furthermore, when using is, there are limited security and guarantee. Because it mostly operates online, it is expected to suffer technical flaws of all sorts, and it is still evolving.

1. Lack of understanding of cryptocurrencies Many people are still unaware of the world of digital currency and the promise it holds. This is comparable to when credit card use was first revealed, and the reaction to it was somewhat close to cryptocurrency. Back then, people wouldn't even believe it was possible to pay for things using a mere coin, yet a whole new digital currency alone.

Since it's unique, and it doesn't directly involve cash, people shy away from it and continuously question its effectiveness. It also requires online access to make it work. Most people think it's easy to have to pay for things or transfer money online and catch on, but some people are still cynical about it.

People need to be educated about it so they can integrate it into their everyday lives to make cryptocurrency acceptable around us. But it requires a lot of energy and time to learn a whole new currency world. Most would think their time isn't worth it because it's still not commonly known.

Although some businesses accept Bitcoins, compared with traditional currencies, the list is significantly small. This probably is because of a lack of knowledge. It is important to inform both companies and consumers. Imagine having to teach your clients a new way to pay for something. This will take a more extended amount of time and effort.

2. Lack of consumer protection and guarantee central banks govern the authority of a nation's money in the case of traditional currency. No higher power will suddenly decide that without protest and dismissal, they no longer wish to use the currency of their country for trade. There are procedures

to follow, paper records, permits, and plenty of other guidelines to follow.

That isn't the case for our digital currency, however. There is no Central Bank that regulates Bitcoin, meaning that nobody can guarantee their minimum value.

For example, the value of Bitcoin would fall dramatically should a large group of merchants decide to' discard' Bitcoins and leave the system. This will inevitably leave other users in a significant loss situation who have invested thousands of dollars in Bitcoins. To claim those expenses, there is no one to call or regulations to help compensate them.

Another reason is that if you get paid but don't get online movie tickets or flight tickets, you can always contact the bank service provider or go to the actual bank and report your case instead. If you pay via Visa and can prove that you have not received your service, then your money will be returned by the credit card company. For a course that was not offered, someone paying £ 2,000–the guy just ran away with their money. Visa fully compensated them for having used their credit card. Even at the time, it was pretty impressive and appalled, as one can imagine other people putting false claims into it.

That is not how cryptocurrency works. First of all, there's no bank in this currency to trade and support you. There is no number you may call and ask someone or email address to talk to.

So, if, for example, you purchased your goods using Bitcoins and the seller didn't send the things you ordered, there's nothing you can do to undo the purchase or refund. You cannot complain in this regard to the police or any relevant authority.

Cryptocurrency transactions tend not to be reversible. Once the money has been sent to an account, you cannot get it back.

And make sure you double-check that you send the coins to the correct address and in the correct currency.

So, the very attraction of Bitcoin's decentralized system is a double-edged sword.

3. Technical shortcomings the possibility of a sudden server failure, power shortage, and even hardware lags was always present as online banking made its way into our lives.

Compared to data corruption or virus infections, your Bitcoin is lost forever if your hard drive crashes and your wallet file gets corrupted. Nothing can be done to restore it, and the mechanism can' orphan' those' coins.'

So, remember, always make a backup to avoid that happening.

4. The industry is still evolving. We are vulnerable to many threats as they are still developing. There are so many unfinished features that can be changed, but finalizing them takes a longer time, particularly if they don't have a physical form.

For traditional currency, with the online payment system, and without us ever seeing the real money being moved from one account to another, at the end of the day, we still end up holding the physical cash. We can use physical cash to physically and digitally buy stuff from the shops.

Because cryptocurrency has no physical form, i.e., we will never carry the physical cash, and its use is limited.

It is more often than not–and I hope this change soon–but to appreciate its worth, Bitcoin needs to be converted to traditional currency.

6.3 The future of cryptocurrency and SEED VENTURE case study

It has been said that these digital currencies will capture the world of online finance. With the blockchain technology behind it, cryptocurrency's future exhibits enormous potential.

Although the process behind Ether prohibits it from being used as a means of direct payment, a bright future for this crypto-currency seems to lie ahead. This is all due to its definition of smart contracts.

On the other hand, cryptocurrencies that solve the privacy problem are beginning to gain more prominent popularity among users.

Bitcoin's rising acceptance level takes the alternative currency to the mainstream. Many companies are considering investing in this currency, driving their path to the financial currency world further.

When institutional money enters the market, some economic analysts predict a significant change in cryptography is coming. There is the possibility of floating crypto on the Nasdaq, which would further give prestige to blockchain and its applications as an alternative to traditional currencies. Many expect that a checked exchange-traded fund (ETF) is all that crypto wants. An ETF would render Bitcoin investing easier for people, but they still need to be the desire to want to spend in cryptography, which some say may not be created automatically with a fund.

Some of the drawbacks currently faced by cryptocurrencies–such as the possibility that a computer crash may delete one's digital wealth, or that a hacker may ransack a virtual vault–can be solved in time by technological advances. What will be harder to overcome is a simple paradox that surrounds cryptocurrencies–the more familiar they are, the more they are likely to attract enforcement and government scrutiny, which erodes the fundamental premise for their existence.

Although the number of merchants who embrace cryptocurrencies has increased steadily, they are still very much in the minority. To order for cryptocurrencies to be used more widely, they must first achieve widespread market acceptance. Nonetheless, their relative novelty compared to traditional currencies, except for the technically advanced, would likely discourage most citizens.

A cryptocurrency that strives to become part of the cultural, financial system may allow widely different requirements to be followed. It'd have to be mathematically complex (to prevent fraud and hacker attacks) but easy to understand for consumers; decentralized but with sufficient customer protections and protection; and maintain user privacy without being a tax evasion platform, money laundering, and other nefarious activities. Since these are formidable requirements to fulfill, is it likely that in a few years, the most common cryptocurrency could have attributes falling between heavily-regulated fiat currencies and the cryptocurrencies today? While that possibility seems remote, there is little doubt that Bitcoin's success (or lack of it) in coping with the challenges it faces may decide the fortunes of other cryptocurrencies in the years ahead, as the leading cryptocurrency at present.

Will one day we be witnessing a new currency norm through cryptocurrency? Researchers concluded that forecasting it would still be too early, yet one thing is sure, that this currency is gradual.

The technologically savvy individuals would be the most targeted group of all, and most of us are already part of that group. Lower than 50 percent of our time is spent online, and this number is increasing.

Someday, for a more convenient transaction, we might even consider using crypto-currency as our standard currency.

SEED Venture:

SEED Venture is a tokenization tool for Venture Capital, financing and the presidium of start-ups through Venture Incubators SEED Venture is an open-source platform based on blockchain technology which provides mechanisms for Financing of new innovative First Phase (so-called' seed stage'), limiting risks and following growth step by step. The funds are allocated directly to start-ups and used to meet the specified milestones; a program is a tracking tool that allows help during the whole early-stage (3-5 years) period. Every completed project would bring value to the investors who took part in it.

SEED Venture is the place where founders, incubators, and start-ups can meet and connect, reducing risks and exchanging goals, giving space to the ecosystem's potential, so that no good idea goes to waste.

It is a venture capital tokenization network that:

- makes private equity fully liquid
- opens the possibility of investing in innovation
- removes barriers
- reduces time
- removes unnecessary intermediaries and costs
- offers new tools to all game players while staying within reach of the respective jurisdictions.

This scheme can be applied by leveraging the potential of blockchain technology, but it does not need to be familiar with its more complicated aspects. This ensures such versatility that incubators operating in different countries can implement their business model following their jurisdictional laws.

Furthermore, start-up companies do not inherently have to be rooted in the cryptocurrency or blockchain world: they may take advantage of this technology when belonging to conventional industries or business models.

SEED Venture provides an environment where members can innovate themselves and their position in the business. Investors may benefit from the tokenization opportunity and function in previously impossible ways. Incubators can help with longer horizons to the growth of start-ups. From the very beginning, start-ups will be sponsored and will be able to deliver on the market their best and attract investors.

SEED Venture is a blockchain-based platform utilizing various tokens within its ecosystem.

"SEED" is the native token that allows investors to fund the start-up pools of incubators. Each incubator shall use its token for the pool. An internal peer-to-peer trading platform will always enable the exchange between the native SEED token and the pool tokens. Automatic smart-contracts can handle the transfer of tokens between the different operators, ensuring transparency and legitimacy.

How do those elements work together?

In a few sample passages let us make this clear:

•investors receive SEED tokens;

•after applying, they are rewarded by the incubators and choose the pools they want to invest in;

•they look at the start-ups in the pool in which they invest;

•the nurseries buy shares, previously agreed, of the start-ups, they are proposing; •investors grant SEED tokens to a smart contract financing

Let us note that the SEED token is not a token of equity: it does not represent the property of the legal entity that launches the platform, nor of the incubators that will use it (which will issue its token as planned), nor of the start-ups that will represent the pool of projects to be supported.

The SEED token gives voting rights to determine a list of start-ups that are most worthy of support, but in no way gives voting rights relevant to majority/minority ownership interests, these will never be exercised via the SEED toke.

Last but not least, the SEED token does not grant rights to token holders nor to those who use the network.

SEED Venture is a network that aims to create an ecosystem in the field of seed funding that promotes new innovative and transformative ventures or programs, a platform that builds on an underlying technology that needs to be considered experimental yet. There may be severe threats (and potential gains).

6.4 Is it too late to get into cryptocurrencies – have you missed the boat

Although making 10,000 percent on the larger coins might be too late, it is still very early, and new inventions, coins, and ideas are being produced almost daily. We are just at the beginning. There will be no question that there will be NEW cryptos, which will also have meteoric rises you can get into. Some were not even invented yet. Anything can happen. Engage in.

Whether you are in the market and can buy on time is quite another thing, so do your homework and get started.

The entire generation looks to Bitcoin as a value shop. The confidence is in the blockchain's decentralized system, which makes breaking into it so tricky. Anyone under the age of 30 considers that Bitcoin makes total sense.

Just thousands of people own any Bitcoin or a fraction of a Bitcoin. This is close to when an iPhone was only available to hundreds of thousands of people. Real growth came when everyone started adopting it, and then it developed into the great millions. So, get in really, before the early adoption starts.

Simon Dixon, co-founder and CEO of BNK to the Future says he saw five waves of cryptocurrencies:

1. The first wave was Bitcoin, which had value because it was a money store independent of a central bank.

2. The second was the Altcoins, in which people tried to copy Bitcoin. Some of them, like Litecoin and Dash, did succeed.

3. You then had shares in businesses, like the Kraken and Coinbase exchanges.

4. Instead, as they are called, there were Tokens or' ICOs,' where companies create an asset class that trades on a secondary market.

5. The last one is' Fork's–where people have disputes about how things should be done and break off, including Ethereum Classic split off from Ethereum and Bitcoin Cash and Bitcoin Gold split off from Bitcoin for example.

6.5 Can crypto save the world

Crypto-currency has many opponents. Others say all of this is an exaggeration. Okay, I got some bad news for those guys. Cryptocurrency is here to stay and will make a better place for the world.

We've been let down by centralized organizations.

• Banks cost taxpayers trillions of dollars in 2008 and caused the world economy to collapse.

- In 2017 the credit inspection agency Equifax lost more than 140,000,000 of the personal details of its customers.

- Facebook was forced to apologize this year for selling private data of its users.

Cryptocurrencies provide another option for people around the world.

The Syrian, Yemen, and Libyan governments have all failed to protect their citizens from brutal civil wars.

What is the crypto-currency for the Syrian people? That is hope. Thirty percent of UN Aid is diverted to corruption by third parties, so UNICEF has used Ethereum to raise money for Syria's children.

About 2 billion people worldwide don't have bank accounts. One in ten Afghanis, many of them women, are unbanked. What is Afghani woman's crypto-currency? It's Freedom. Bitcoin is giving women financial freedom for the first time in Afghanistan.

Blockchain technology might be used in some of the world's most corrupt countries to run for elections.

7: Conclusion

You've studied what cryptocurrencies are and how they have functioned to date. You know how to store it, and where to sell it. Comprehending cryptocurrencies, however, is more than just knowing blockchains and mining. Understanding cryptocurrency is about understanding what you can do with those technologies.

In short, cryptocurrencies continue to evolve. Regulators are still figuring out how to safeguard crypto investors in many countries. Several countries have been open to the idea of embracing cryptocurrencies, while others have discouraged them. Bitcoin is legal in the United States, Canada, Australia, and some EU (European Union) nations, including Germany, the UK, Belgium, and others. Nations such as China, Russia, India, and some South American countries, on the other hand, are against Bitcoin use.

Bitcoin tax can be paid if you use a good exchange and keep track of your trades. It would be best if you calculated every single profit, not only from trading but also from using Bitcoins to make things pay.

But that is just the start. When it comes to Altcoins, things are a confusing nightmare. The Altcoin works for the tax authorities, just like Bitcoin. This means that in most countries, it is not a financial product, but instead property. You have to tax the difference if you buy it with Bitcoin and sell it for Bitcoin, but not in Bitcoin, but Dollar or your federal paper money. It means you don't just need to keep track of all your Altcoin trades, but also take into account Bitcoin's price when buying and selling.

Bitcoin's introduction has engendered a discussion about its existence and that of other cryptocurrencies. Despite the recent problems with Bitcoin, its popularity since its official release in 2009, alternative cryptocurrencies such as Litecoin, Ripple, and MintChip were inspired to be created. A cryptocurrency seeking to become part of the mainstream financial system would have to follow very different requirements. While that possibility seems distant, there is little doubt that the success or failure of Bitcoin in overcoming the challenges it faces that decide the fortunes of other cryptocurrencies in the years ahead.

In the global financial system, the cryptocurrencies are a hot topic. Cryptocurrencies' exchange rates are incredibly unpredictable. There is a high risk of exchanging such cryptocurrencies with this. Their development has drawn many speculators' attention.

They are easy to carry. It will only be used on a broader scale after the appropriate confidence in the cryptocurrencies. If the cryptocurrencies fail to gain trust, then their boom can decline. They're still in their infancy, and it's not clear when they're going to be traded internationally in mature markets. Several different cryptocurrencies got the publicity needed. Several nations have already begun releasing national cryptocurrencies.

It is quite likely that for cryptocurrencies to thrive early, the bitcoins might have away. Despite the flaws, the digital currency still finds Bitcoins to be tour-de-force. This provided the less developed countries with alternative money and opened the doors to economic change. This offers individuals more opportunities to manage their finances in this way. Without regard to the bitcoins executing the elevated transformations, the cryptocurrencies are seen to enter the financial stage and forever change the global economic landscape.

Digital and democratized cryptocurrencies have the ability in the very distant future to replace government-backed fiat currencies as the primary means of making financial transactions. With that in mind, Microsoft has also begun to promote large-scale simulation research in the name of banks and other large corporations interested in understanding the possible consequences of such a widespread change in the global economy. We will help you take control of your money and information back with you. Some people are going to ignore them and hope that they are going away. Others are joining the party. Which one are you going to be?

8: References

What is Cryptocurrency: Cryptocurrency Explained the Easy Way Retrieved from https://www.bitdegree.org/tutorials/what-is-cryptocurrency/#Crypto_Definition

Understanding Cryptocurrency Market Cap. Retrieved from https://www.coinist.io/cryptocurrency-market-cap/

List of top virtual crypto currencies in Retrieved from https://www.businessinsider.com/top-cryptocurrencies

What is Cryptocurrency? - CryptoGround. Retrieved from https://www.cryptoground.com/guide/what-is-cryptocurrency#What-is-Cryptocurrency?

Cryptocurrency Trading: Everything You Need to Know! Retrieved from https://www.bitdegree.org/tutorials/cryptocurrency-trading/#Cryptocurrency_Trading

Blenkinsop, C. Crypto Trading, Explained. Retrieved from https://cointelegraph.com/explained/crypto-trading-explained

What is cryptocurrency trading and how does it work? Retrieved from https://www.ig.com/ae/cryptocurrency-trading/what-is-cryptocurrency-trading-how-does-it-work

About Mark

Mark Archer writes books, which, considering where you're reading this, makes perfect sense. He's best known for writing about no-finction on subjects ranging from personal finance to astronomy to film, was the Digital Consultant for two big US Corporate of IT. He enjoys pie, as should all right thinking people. You can get to his blog by typing the word "Mark Archer" into Google. No, seriously, try it.
Keep in touch with Mark via twitter @MarkArc83438720 and subscribe his newsletter here https://mrcl74.wixsite.com/markarcher

Printed in Great Britain
by Amazon